Visioning and Visualization

Visioning and Visualization

People, Pixels, and Plans

Michael Kwartler and Gianni Longo

LINCOLN INSTITUTE
OF LAND POLICY
CAMBRIDGE, MASSACHUSETTS

Library of Congress Cataloging-in-Publication Data

Kwartler, Michael.

  Visioning and visualization : people, pixels, and plans / by Michael
Kwartler and Gianni Longo.

     p. cm.

  Includes bibliographical references and index.

  ISBN 978-1-55844-180-4

  1. Land use—Planning—Computer simulation. 2. Land
use—Planning—Citizen participation. 3. Land use—United
States—Planning—Case studies. 4. Information visualization.
I. Longo, Gianni, 1947- II. Lincoln Institute of Land Policy. III. Title.

  HD108.6.K95 2008

  333.730285--dc22

                          2008008178

Designed by Peter M. Blaiwas, Vern Associates, Inc.

Composed in Frutiger. Printed and bound by Capital Offset Company in Concord, New Hampshire.
The paper is Galerie Art silk, a recycled sheet.

MANUFACTURED IN UNITED STATES OF AMERICA

Front cover: An eye-level view of Broadway in the 3D physical model used for visualizing a zoning alternative. The scale is revealed by the person's hand inserting an object into the model. (Environmental Simulation Center, 1993)

Back cover: Two screen shots from an interactive real-time 3D model used during the design phase of the Greenwich Street South Urban Design Plan. The top image shows existing conditions—the Brooklyn-Battery Tunnel entrance and a parking structure spanning the approach. The bottom image shows the proposed alternative, which decks over the tunnel entrance, replaces the garage with a park and new residential towers, and restores the historic street system, which was interrupted by the tunnel entrance. The ability to move freely in the virtual environment proved invaluable in understanding complex design issues and spatial relationships. (Environmental Simulation Center, 2004)

Title page: During one of several workshops held throughout the Ohio, Kentucky, and Indiana region surrounding the city of Cincinnati, participants developed growth scenarios that were subsequently calibrated and digitized to identify areas of consensus. (ACP–Visioning & Planning)

Contents

Figures

Boxes

Acknowledgments

We thank the Lincoln Institute of Land Policy for its generous funding of this book, which has its roots in the many Lincoln Institute–sponsored Visioning and Visualization workshops that we have conducted across the country. Special thanks go to Armando Carbonell, who conceived both the need for the workshops and the idea for this book. Thanks also to Lisa Cloutier who has been instrumental in making the Visioning and Visualization courses as successful as they have been. We deeply appreciate Lincoln Institute's Ann LeRoyer and Brian Hotchkiss of Vern Associates for their gracious support, gentle prodding, and insightful editing as we produced this manuscript. And finally the book's designer, Peter Blaiwas of Vern Associates, has crafted a volume that is able to clearly and elegantly communicate our ideas to the reader.

The architects, planners, and landscape architects at the Environmental Simulation Center (ESC) have all contributed to the development and application of the visual simulation tools described in the manuscript. In particular, we thank Paul Patnode for his tireless dedication and genius for translating innovative concepts into reality as represented in the graphics that illuminate the manuscript. Paul and the ESC staff, including Alihan Polat, Kiyoshi Yamazaki, and Prasanta Bhattarai, have created, refined, and assembled the book's graphics.

Several members of the staff at ACP–Visioning & Planning have provided tremendous support in refining the visioning process and in helping with this manuscript. Jamie Greene, ACP's principal, has provided encouragement and advice from the start. Suzanne Nienaber has contributed to the writing and editing of this text, helping to weave together its many parts. Jennifer Lindbom has polished ACP's public process guidelines and trained untold numbers of facilitators in cities throughout the country. Greta Stough and Daria Siegel have provided logistical support to the manuscript's final production.

—Michael Kwartler, Environmental Simulation Center
—Gianni Longo, ACP–Visioning & Planning

Introduction

The purpose of *Visioning and Visualization* is to assist urban professionals, public sector leaders, and the public to navigate two complex and evolving fields: public involvement and digital visualization as applied to planning. To that end, this book is based on the authors' experiences in developing sophisticated public involvement processes and applying information technology to planning and design.

Two remarkable phenomena have affected the practice of planning over the past two decades: the rise of public involvement as an integral component of urban decision making and the technological innovations that enable the visualization and simulation of physical reality. Together the two phenomena anticipate the future, turning the planning process into a journey of discovery for professionals and laypeople alike.

The book is not a "how to" publication. It does not focus on the procedural steps of public process techniques or on specific technical features of digital visualization tools. Rather, the book suggests ways that digital visualization tools can be integrated in a public process to offer participants clear choices and help them make informed planning decisions. Evidence from communities throughout the country shows that public involvement supported by visualization leads to better plans and more livable communities.

The book is organized in six chapters:

- *Chapter 1,* "The Context," presents a historic overview of the public involvement and digital visualization fields. It traces the trajectory of public involvement in planning from confrontational and adversarial tactics to the present emphasis on cooperation and inclusion. It expands on the evolution of representation techniques from perspective drawings to computer-aided visual simulations.

- *Chapter 2,* "Benefits, Principles, and Lessons Learned," outlines principles to guide the integration of public process and visualization tools in a democratic decision-making process. It also explores lessons learned in the application of digital visualization tools to planning activities.

- *Chapter 3,* "Public Involvement Techniques in Planning," illustrates visions, charrettes, and other techniques that invite the use of visualization tools.

- *Chapter 4,* "Visual Simulation Tools," introduces specific tools and their uses in planning, including representing existing conditions, visualizing alternatives, and monitoring impacts.

- *Chapter 5,* "Implementation," describes formal and informal ways the implementation of a plan can benefit from feedback opportunities created by visualization tools.

- *Chapter 6,* "Case Studies," presents four case studies spanning from the regional to the neighborhood scale where public involvement and visualization tools were used to help the public make informed decisions.

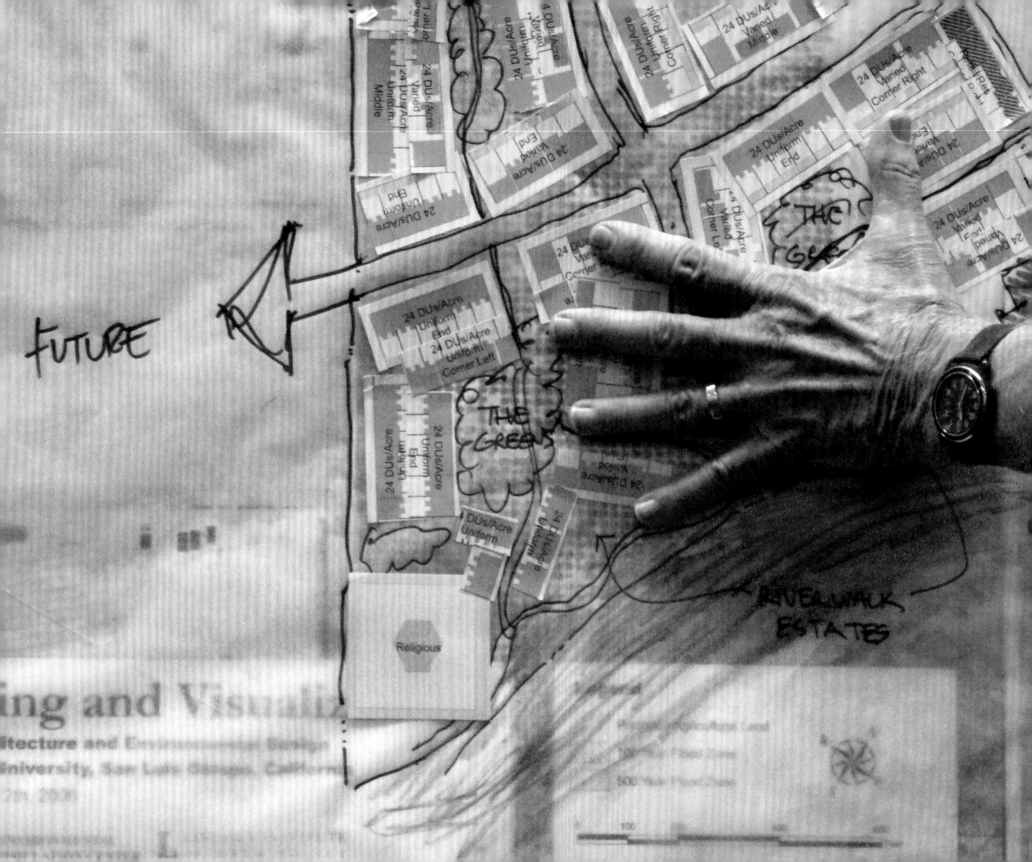

1. The Context

FROM CONFRONTATION TO COOPERATION

The direct involvement of the public in contributing to making decisions that affect our cities and regions is not a new phenomenon. It finds its roots in the earliest form of democracy of the Greek city-states and was a strong component of the civic foundation of this nation. Over time, however, direct involvement of citizens in the affairs of a city has declined. By 1961, as Jane Jacobs (figure 1.1) succinctly wrote in *The Death and Life of Great American Cities,* there were "only two ultimate public powers in shaping and running American cities: votes and control of the money" (Jacobs 1993, 171).

In this environment the public was by and large cut off from directly participating and having a say in shaping cities. Opportunities for providing input were typically limited to very formal public hearings, intimidating affairs held in formal chambers, where "helplessness, and its partner, futility, became almost palpable" (Jacobs 1993, 529).

Figure 1.1 – Jane Jacobs (Image courtesy of Frank Lennon / *Toronto Star*)

Proxy chips representing 3D building blocks are used to build a development scenario and evaluate its performance in a real-time 3D model. Visioning and Visualization Workshop cosponsored by the Lincoln Institute of Land Policy and the College of Architecture and Environmental Design at California Polytechnic State University at San Luis Obispo. (ACP–Visioning & Planning)

Although marginalized at the public hearing, the public was not silent. Jane Jacobs describes the "abounding vitality, earnestness and sense with which so many of the citizens [participating in public hearings] rise to the occasion. Very plain people including the poor, including the discriminated against, including the uneducated, reveal themselves momentarily as people with grains of greatness in them, and I do not speak sardonically" (Jacobs 1993, 529). The vitality and earnestness of the public were about to transform the formal civility of the public hearing into confrontation.

In the aftermath of World War II, the federal government engaged in massive investments in housing, transportation, and social programs. Yet those programs often necessitated large-scale relocation and the breakdown of viable neighborhoods. These were conditions that forced a bottom-up direct involvement of citizens and neighborhood groups.

A major target for civic opposition was the massive federal urban highway program. As a direct result of that program, in the early 1960s cities began to clear wide swaths of land, mostly in inner cities and poor neighborhoods. Cities were hacking their way, in Robert Moses's words, "with a meat ax" (Heckscher 1977, 119). Neighborhood residents in New York, Phoenix, and Baltimore, among many other cities, rebelled against heavy-handed programs, stopped construction of proposed highways altogether, or demanded and obtained more suitable alternatives.

Confrontational tactics against urban renewal projects worked equally well in efforts to preserve unique features of a community and followed a similar script. The City of Seattle proposed a 220-acre urban renewal project that would raze Pike Place Market and areas surrounding it. Citizens organized as Friends of the Market and gathered 50,000 signatures on a petition to declare the market a historic district. In spite of opposition from the city, the business community, and the local newspapers, when the petition was put to a vote, citizens voted overwhelmingly to protect the market.

At about the same time in the 1960s, neighborhoods began to organize to address compelling issues of social and environmental justice. Community organizing was not a new phenomenon. In the 1930s, Saul Alinsky had organized the Back of the Yards, an industrial and residential neighborhood located on the southwest side of Chicago, which was profiled in Upton Sinclair's 1906 book *The Jungle* (Sinclair 2004). Alinsky's work in the Back of the Yards neighborhood became a model and an inspiration. Assisted by the training and organizing

work of the Industrial Area Foundation (founded by Alinsky) and other capacity-building groups, countless community organizations sprang up throughout the country. Alinsky's activism fueled the reemergence of the public as a key participant in the decision-making process.

The 1970s saw the emergence of business as a third power base in the urban decision-making arena. Business, of course, had always played an important role in civic affairs. Great examples of such involvement are the forward-looking 1906 Plan for Chicago sponsored by the Commercial Club (a business organization) and the activities of the Allegheny Conference in Pittsburgh after World War II.

In the 1970s businesses began to invest substantial resources in addressing specific problems and challenges. The Greater Baltimore Committee, for example, led the redevelopment of Baltimore's Inner Harbor, which became an exemplar of successful inner-city revitalization. Seattle METRO, having spectacularly succeeded in cleaning the waters of Lake Washington, focused on an ambitious program of park, transportation, and other quality of life initiatives called Forward Thrust. These initiatives were the result of the vision and leadership of inspired individuals. It is a tribute to these leaders' focus and intensity that their top-down approach succeeded as well as it did.

A CENTER-OUT APPROACH TO DECISION MAKING

By the early 1980s the question in the minds of many was how to bring together government, business, and the public in ways that would not be confrontational and that would lead to cooperation and, more importantly, to support during implementation. In other words, how to build Senator Bill Bradley's "three-legged stool," which included government and the private sector as two of the legs and civil society as the third (*New York Times* 1995).

The establishment of the government, business, and civic triad as an effective way to do business in cities and, increasingly, regionally has not displaced confrontation entirely. In fact, such displacement would not be desirable, as debate on issues continues and changes over time. Confrontation today, in the form of NIMBYism (the not in my back yard type of activism), remains very much a part of the shaping of cities and regions. However, an open and inclusive public involvement approach to address issues will reduce the chances that opposition flares up, since projects and initiatives are amply debated in the community, within established criteria, and principles are developed that the community agrees to uphold.

The experiences of some of the most progressive cities showed that the answer to the "three-legged stool" question was to seek a new model of urban decision making based neither on a bottom-up nor a top-down approach. In hindsight it seems entirely logical that the model to emerge would be one that brings the broadest range of interests to the table—in other words, an all-inclusive, center-out approach.

Vision 2000 in Chattanooga, Tennessee, was one of the first planning processes to aim for such an approach. At a time when most efforts were still top-down or bottom-up, Vision 2000 recognized the need to expand the circle of inclusiveness. In 1984, just a few months after its start, the program had ensured the direct involvement of business and government leaders, foundations, educational institutions, the clergy, arts and other special interest groups, and citizens. They agreed to participate in the actual process of developing a shared agenda and pledged to stay involved through developing a vision and implementation. "We wanted people who were both hopeful and helpful," said Mai Bell Hurley, the chair of Chattanooga Venture (the organization set up to be the recipient of Vision 2000).

The coming together of all these forces propelled the community on a trajectory of implementation successes that it still follows today, 23 years later (box 1.1). Chattanooga has become a sought-after destination for delegations from cities throughout the country that are eager to understand and imitate its success. In its May 1998 issue, the magazine *Governing* stated that "visioning fever" is "a very contagious bug that has been sweeping civic America in the late 1990s," due in part to the success of Vision 2000 (Walters 1998).

Inclusive models of public involvement proliferated through the 1990s as a result of numerous factors. One of them was Community Partnership Strategy, a key priority of the U.S. Department of Housing and Urban Development during the Clinton administration, which required inclusive participation as a precondition to funding. Another resulted from the rise of metropolitan regions. As cities grew beyond their jurisdictional boundaries, regions became de facto cities, the places where people lived, worked, shopped, and recreated. Regions, however, are complex multijurisdictional realities. In regions, inclusive and comprehensive public involvement programs became the preferred, and often the only, way to develop shared regional agendas with enough public support to be implemented.

Box 1.1 **The Chattanooga Story**

In the early 1980s, Chattanooga, Tennessee, suffered from a number of problems that had been building for a long time. In 1969, the Environmental Protection Agency declared that Chattanooga had the worst air quality of any urban area in the United States. Unemployment was at a historic high. The transformation from a manufacturing base to a service economy was lagging due to the lack of an adequately prepared workforce. Race relations were stressed and erupted in violence in 1981.

Trying to respond to these problems and driven by a desire to develop a clear agenda for the future of the community, a number of civic leaders came together and sought to take action outside the political arena. These individuals became the first ring (core) of participants in the center-out approach. During a visit to Indianapolis in spring 1983, these community leaders became acquainted with the Greater Indianapolis Progress Committee (GIPC). Upon returning, they began to meet weekly in an open-salon manner in a vacant storefront. More residents joined in, forming the second ring of participants. These meetings were passionate, heady, engaging, risk taking, and rigorous. By everyone's admission, nothing like it had ever occurred in Chattanooga. These informal meetings led to several critical decisions:

- An organization—loosely modeled after GIPC, and later called Chattanooga Venture—would be formed.
- Chattanooga Venture would develop a citywide agenda through a public involvement process (Vision 2000).
- The process would be inclusive and transparent and would start with a blank slate with no predetermined issue.
- The discussion would be organized under general headings such as people, place, play, jobs, government, and "future alternatives," a catch-all heading for any idea that did not fit the other categories.
- The circle of participants would be enlarged to include business, government, foundations, special interest groups, citizens, and anyone willing to contribute time and ideas to the process. (This became a cast of thousands as the participation rings enlarged.)
- The governance structure of Chattanooga Venture would reflect the makeup of the community and the circle of participants.
- Participants would pledge to become involved in implementing Vision 2000's agenda.

Because there were no precedents and the outcomes were unknown, these decisions had a high-risk aura at the time, but have since become the paradigm for this type of public involvement process.

Chattanooga Venture, with funding from the Lyndhurst Foundation (a local foundation that played a leading role in implementation), conducted Vision 2000 in a period of eight months, from fall 1983 to spring 1984. Implementation started in earnest thereafter. Vision 2000's success was extraordinary. It became the catalyst for the coming together of the public, private, and civic sectors in implementing forty shared goals and objectives to cover areas such as downtown revitalization, the riverfront, human relations, education, affordable housing, jobs, and the city's form of government. In the first ten years, it prompted 223 projects and initiatives that created thousands of permanent and temporary construction jobs, and stimulated more than $1 billion in investments (figure 1.2).

Vision 2000 drastically changed the way business was conducted in Chattanooga because it demonstrated, without qualifications, that transparency in decision making is an asset that will speed rather than slow implementation (a concern often expressed at the time). It showed that taking risks and being open to new ideas would pay dividends in the form of innovation, which was a key in Chattanooga's success in dealing with seemingly intractable issues such as affordable housing, which was addressed through the highly imitated Chattanooga Neighborhood Enterprise organization. Vision 2000 demonstrated vividly that rekindling citizenship and encouraging participation, not just with ideas but also with direct involvement in implementation, can be a rewarding, creative, and fun activity. Not incidentally, three citizens—a planning professional and two business leaders—have since run for office and have been repeatedly elected as councilpersons and mayor, further integrating their leadership in Vision 2000 with their work in government.

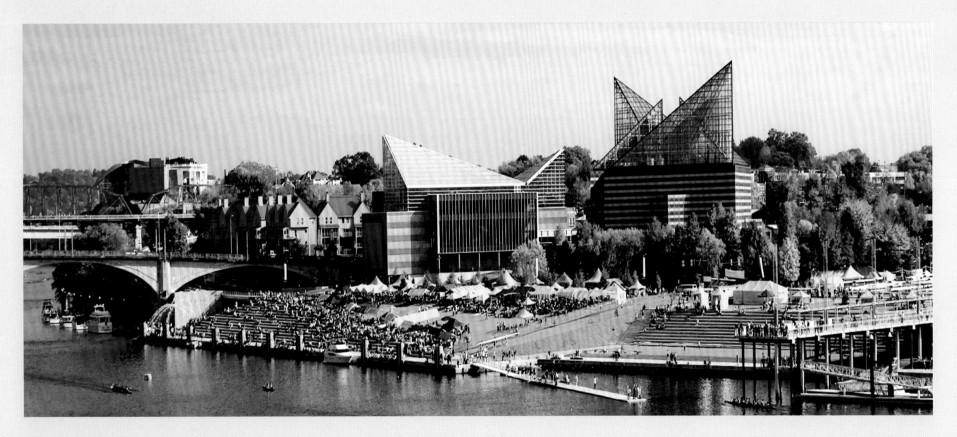

Figure 1.2 – The Tennessee Aquarium in Chattanooga has been the catalyst for the riverfront development and has become the symbol of the city's renaissance. It is the focal point of the Riverbend Festival, the city's largest community event. (Image courtesy RiverCity Company)

SEEING TO UNDERSTAND THE WORLD

Visual simulation is a form of representation in which things that do not exist, but are contemplated, are represented or simulated allowing the user virtually to peer into the future. Until the advent of the motion picture, visual simulations were two-dimensional (2D) images (e.g., an architect's renderings of yet-to-be-built buildings). Current technology allows us to create three-dimensional (3D) virtual reality environments in which the user is an active participant, determining where she is going and what she is looking at in the 3D virtual model. These types of virtual environments are also referred to as immersive environments or real-time environments because the user controls the experience of actually moving around in the 3D model.

Visual simulation in a 3D virtual reality environment has a long pedigree in the history of visual representation. The change in representation of places from the medieval quasi-axonometric view (figure 1.3) to the Renaissance system of linear perspective (figure 1.4) was not only a shift in representation, but a profound philosophical change in how people perceived themselves in the world. In Lorenzetti's frescos, the representation of the world is not based on the location of the painter—it is as if from God's view, if you will. This view is supplanted by the Renaissance homocentric view of the world in which the

Figure 1.3 – Ambrogio Lorenzetti, *Effects of Good Government on City Life* (detail), 1338–1340, illustrates the medieval quasi-axonometric view. (Photo Credit: Erich Lessing / Art Resource, NY)

Figure 1.4 – Luciano Laurana, *Ideal City,* 15th century, illustrates linear perspective developed by Florentine architect Brunelleschi. (Photo Credit: Scala / Art Resource, NY)

Figure 1.5 – Albrecht Dürer, *Draughtsman Drawing a Recumbent Woman*, 1525, illustrates the perceiver's point of view. Woodcut illustration from *The Teaching of Measurements.* (Photo Credit: Foto Marburg / Art Resource, NY)

painter, the perceiver, becomes the critical element in representation; hence, the term point of view (figure 1.5).

The representational convention of reality in linear perspective is about the "accurate" placement of objects as perceived by a single viewer from a single location at a single moment in time. If the viewer moved, the perceived placement of objects would change as well. The representations were static, since only one point of view could be represented at a time. Advances using the camera obscura added a new element of naturalism to the representation of places—such as those seen in city views painted by Canaletto in Italy and England and by Vermeer in Holland (figure 1.6). Later artists attempted to bring representation closer to the human physiology of seeing by using the optical lens as a proxy for the human eye.

In the nineteenth and twentieth centuries the advancement of the camera and the science of human physiology and perception led to dramatic changes in representation. With the advent of photography, painting no longer needed to be tied to recording events or making "naturalistic representations," but was freed to explore how we see and perceive the world around us. The innovations of Manet and Cézanne through those of David Hockney are profound examples of the shift from realism to the physiology and psychology of human perception. Nonetheless, the images remained static representations, at best implying motion, time, and change (figure 1.7). Film and animation provided the means to capture those aspects, but this was still from the point of view of the lens in an edited, predetermined form in which the viewer passively responds to a controlled flow of visual information.

The innovative use of film to understand how people use space greatly benefited planning and urban design. William H. Whyte, in his film on the Seagram's Building Plaza in New York City, used time-lapse photography to record where,

Figure 1.6 – Camera obscura: a new naturalism. Jan Vermeer van Delft, *View of Delft* (detail), 1660.

Figure 1.7 – In *Place Furstenberg, Paris, August 7, 8, 9, 1985,* David Hockney records his "looking" in separate photographs, consciously imitating the way in which the eye scans an environment. The separate photographs are then assembled into a photomontage. Photographic collage; 43 ½" x 61 ⅜"; © David Hockney, 1985.

how, and at what time of day people used plaza space. The time-lapse film not only revealed that the plaza was well used and inviting, but also provided insights into the nature of and reasons for activity.

Animation provided the means to directly create virtual environments that, nonetheless, still relied on linear perspective and its conventionalized form of representation. It is the precursor to digital visual simulation.

DEVELOPMENTS IN COMPUTER-AIDED DECISION MAKING

Over the past 30 years, computer-assisted planning and urban design have come of age. Beginning in the 1960s, information sciences focused on data and electronic data processing. Later, with information management (management information systems, or MIS) of the 1970s, decision support systems (DSS) in the 1980s, and in the 1990s more comprehensive planning and design decision support systems (PDDSS), information sciences have increasingly been integrated into planning and urban design practice and public decision making.

The growing menu of tools should not blur this critical question: How does one use and integrate these tools in the participatory planning process to improve the public's understanding of the issues and their choices for the future? When used in conjunction with geographic information systems (GIS), impact analysis, and forecasting tools, visual simulation has emerged as one of the most powerful tools to engage citizens and lay decision makers.

The Origins of Geographic Information Systems (GIS)

The development of GIS and the integration of analytical reasoning into GIS have been deeply influenced by the work in the 1960s–1970s of Carl Steinitz at the Harvard University Graduate School of Design and Ian McHarg at the University of Pennsylvania. McHarg's 1969 book, *Design with Nature,* describes a manual geographic information system—GIS before GIS. The subject of the book is ecology, the interplay between natural and man-made systems. For example, by creating separate maps of discrete information on acetate, and overlaying the geo-referenced sheets in logical sequence, McHarg was able to determine what land was not developable by first setting metrics and then sequentially layering data acetates depicting wetlands, slopes, agricultural land, important animal habitats, etc. (McHarg 1969). The resulting map illustrated the places where development would be appropriate.

To get to the output, the user needed to:

- formulate a question or query;

- assemble the data needed to respond to the question;

- determine the variables and formulate criteria to be used to screen the data;

- establish the sequence of analysis most critical to the least critical variables (This is important, as it allows the user to understand the deductive process at each stage in the analysis.); and

- select the appropriate display format or formats.

If done in GIS, McHarg's analysis would result in a series of maps showing the process of deduction, illuminating the relationship among data layers and tabular and graphic information not only about each data layer, but about the results (e.g., how much land is in agricultural use? in critical habitats? on slopes? or less than 2 percent forested? and, in the end, how much land is developable?). The last operation would involve querying the results using GIS's capability to quantify both existing data and the new information created in response to a query.

Digital Visual Simulation and 3D Geographic Information Systems

Digital visual simulation emerged in the 1990s from six different user groups:

1. Digital photomontage from the graphics industry (e.g., the application Photoshop) (figure 1.8)

2. 3D modeling, rendering, and animation from computer-aided drafting (CAD) for architects (e.g., the application 3D Studio) (figure 1.9)

3. 3D graphics from the computer gaming industry (figure 1.10)

4. Animation and digital special effects from the entertainment industry (figure 1.11)

5. Real-time interactive virtual reality 3D environments from the defense industry (figure 1.12)

6. GIS from geography and environmental planning and management (figure 1.13)

Figure 1.8 – A digital photomontage showing before and after conditions of a proposed urban renewal project. The "after" photomontage (below) is created by the artist by adding elements using Adobe Photoshop or other digital image-editing tools. (Images courtesy of Urban Advantage)

Figure 1.9 – A rendered CAD image for the Theater for a New Audience in Brooklyn, New York. All the elements in the scene are modeled with geometry and rendered using materials, textures, lighting effects (including shadows, reflectance, transparency, etc.), and atmospheric effects (sky and haze) to achieve realism. (Image courtesy of H³ Hardy Collaboration Architecture LLC, New York, NY)

While they emerged more or less in the same time frame, each technique was developed to serve a specific purpose driven by the needs of its user group, and for all intents and purposes they were not interchangeable. Their origins not-withstanding, a convergence of visual simulation techniques is now evolving. An early example is the development of 3D GIS that merged CAD 3D representation of a place with attribute data about the place and the objects in it in a format that allowed the user to pose questions (queries) to the database and have the results visualized in three dimensions as well as traditional charts and tables (e.g., Environmental Simulation Center's 3D GIS; figure 1.14). More recently, GIS has been linked to real-time interactive 3D environments by adapting virtual reality real-time formats for its 3D visual simulations. Convergence is also seen in the development PDDSS, where information can be queried and displayed in a multi-dimensional environment.

Visual simulation tools, particularly those that represent the world in an interactive 3D virtual environment, support the planning of places. Of the six

Figure 1.10 – A screen shot from an educational computer video game targeting students 13–19 years old, challenging them to be critical and reflective about real-world conflicts. (Global Conflicts: Palestine 2007; © Serious Games Interactive)

Figure 1.12 – A screen shot from a real-time virtual reality simulation for military flight training. (Image courtesy of Presagis)

Figure 1.11 – A frame from the computer-generated animated movie *Elephants Dream,* the first movie made entirely with open source graphics software. (© 2006, Blender Foundation / Netherlands Media Art Institute)

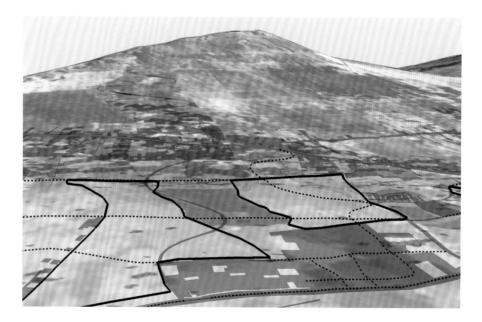

Figure 1.13 – In this example from Kona, Hawaii, steep slopes (red), agricultural lands of significance (green), endangered species habitat (purple), and proximity to existing development (gray) were some of the factors used to delineate areas appropriate for urban expansion (outlined in black). (Environmental Simulation Center, 2006)

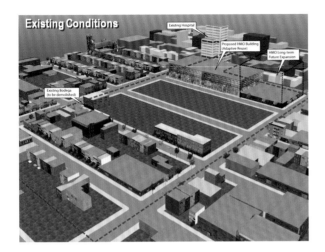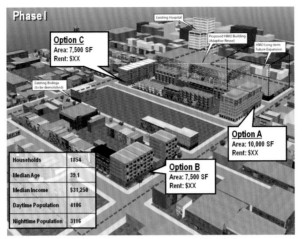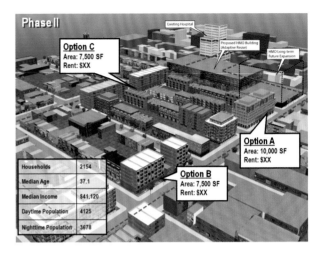

Figures 1.14 – 3D GIS represents a transition from a purely visual display by integrating the 3D model with a queryable database. In this example a store owner in a hypothetical redevelopment area (left) queries the 3D GIS to determine potential relocation sites that will become available at the end of Phase I (middle) as well as the proposed market demographics at the end of Phases I and II (middle and right). (Human Development Overlay District (HDOD): Environmental Simulation Center / Ford Foundation, 2007)

types of tools, GIS is the most familiar to planners. In the world of GIS, analytical graphics and 2D maps were the preferred modes of representation until recently. Connections to other data and databases varied considerably among the other modes. For example, digital photomontages and film or computer-generated animation are purely visual data, while the others have varying capacities to attribute other data and information to the 3D models and environments. GIS has historically had the strongest connection between data and 3D visual simulation because of its origins in geography and as an analytical land and environmental planning tool. What these tools share is their reliance on the representational conventions of mapping, orthographic projections, and linear perspective.

Of the six modes of digital visual simulation, only real-time interactive virtual reality allows the user to navigate freely in a virtual 3D environment. A dividend resulting from the end of the Cold War, real-time interactive virtual reality was used (and today is increasingly used) in flight simulation training and war games. Computer games, while similar, restrict the user to a limited set of options in a narrowly delineated 3D environment, albeit an increasingly complex one. Animation, either in the CAD environment or the entertainment industry, can create hyper-realistic environments in a controlled format that includes a narrative, supported by predetermined paths and editing, that literally frames the viewer's experience. Digital photomontage is similar to animation, predetermining the viewer's visual field, albeit in a static photographic image.

Planning and Design Decision Support Systems (PDDSS)

Planning and design decision support systems are the planning tools of choice as most of them have been specifically designed to be integrated into the public decision-making process. They have the capacity to make sense of complex problems and issues for laypeople and professionals without simplifying or "dumbing" them down. At the moment, two sophisticated PDDSS have emerged that are built on a GIS platform: INDEX (figure 1.15) and CommunityViz™, both of which include powerful 2D and 3D design and visualization tools.

While we will focus on PDDSS, it is important to understand that they are a subset of planning decision support systems (PDSS) and share many but not all of the characteristics of PDSS. For example, most PDSS and PDDSS are built on a GIS platform or on some GIS data, and they support scenario planning where scenarios can be created, and variables and constants can be changed (including spatial configurations such as the allocation of land uses). These systems produce results that can be evaluated against user-determined criteria such as

Visioning and Visualization

performance indicators, benchmarks, and capacities. The defining characteristic of PDDSS is that they are *design* tools.

PDSS models can be categorized as either allocative or sketch models. In allocative models the computer algorithms distribute projected jobs and housing units in the area being planned. In sketch models the user distributes projected jobs and housing units in the area under consideration. Because PDDSS by definition includes design, sketch-based models are the only types of software that let the user design the physical form of a community. Allocative models typically used are:

- METROPILUS (DRAM/EMPAL), which is widely used by regional councils of government (COGs) to allocate employment and households;

- CURBA (California Urban Biodiversity Analysis) models, which factor in ecological considerations;

- UrbanSim, which is used for regional planning, models the relationship between transportation, land use, and the real estate market based on microeconomics; and

- What if?, which allocates land uses based on policies.

Sketch models typically used are:

- CommunityViz™ (designed and developed by the Environmental Simulation Center with Multi-Gen Paradigm, Foresight Consulting, and Pricewater-houseCoopers for the Orton Family Foundation) consists of two components, a scenario constructor and a tool that can be used to design places and visually simulate them in a real-time 3D environment.

- INDEX includes 2D design tools called Paint the Town and Paint the Region. INDEX is similar to CommunityViz's™ scenario constructor allowing for user-determined indicators.

- PLACE³S (Planning for Community Energy, Economic, and Environmental Sustainability) is also a scenario-construction tool with basic 2D mapping capability where plans can be evaluated against indicators that are templates, similar to CommunityViz™ and INDEX.

Three-dimensional planning and urban design tools have a lineage that originated in the early 1980s. The objective of these early tools was to allow stakeholders to experience a streetscape visually by moving through the environment at eye level. These tools emerged from special-effects simulators developed by the film industry and driving/flight simulators. The former involved the construction of physical models at a scale large enough to accommodate an optical probe suspended on a gantry connected to motion-control software that programmed a path through the physical model (figure 1.16).

To make simulation more accessible to laypeople, photographs of existing and proposed buildings were perspective corrected and literally glued to the physical massing model, creating a convincing visual experience (figure 1.17). The path through the model could either be predetermined, as in an animation, or forged manually by the user, who directs the movement of the optical probe through the physical model. The user would experience movement through the physical model on a monitor as it is simultaneously recorded on videotape, from which it

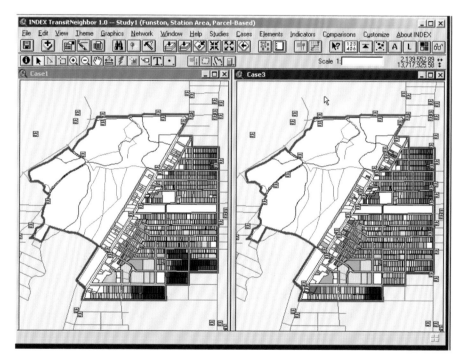

Figure 1.15 – This image illustrates the walkability of two planning scenarios providing different levels of transit service, whereby shades of green indicate parcels with good transit access, and shades of red represent parcels with poor transit access. The scenario on the right adds more transit stops to increase the number of parcels with good transit access. (Image courtesy of Criterion Planners, Inc.)

Figure 1.16 – Visualizing zoning alternatives for Broadway on Manhattan's Upper West Side: Prior to the development of real-time photorealistic 3D digital models, a gantry-mounted miniature camera controlled by computer moves through and records a video on a path in a physical scale model. Photographs of existing and proposed buildings are corrected for parallax and mounted on the physical massing models to create a photo-real effect. (Environmental Simulation Center, 1993)

Figure 1.17 – An eye-level view of Broadway in the 3D physical model used for visualizing a zoning alternative. The scale of the model is revealed by the person's hand inserting an object into the model. (Environmental Simulation Center, 1993)

could be shown, independent of the gantry, on a videocassette recorder. Alternatives could be inserted into the 3D model at preselected points in the walk-through or recorded separately along the same path and compared by splitting the screen into multiple windows and viewing the alternatives simultaneously and in synchronization with each other.

Concurrently, immersive interactive digital environments were being developed for the driving/flight simulation industry. Similar to visual simulation, which employed physical models and moving optical probes, these environments also required a high degree of visual realism to make them effective teaching and learning tools. Rather than paste photographs on a physical model, this software pasted photographs of buildings and landscape on virtual 3D massing models of buildings and topography.

The visual effect was similar to that of physical simulators, with two distinct differences. First, it was immersive, allowing the user to navigate freely and easily and respond in real time without prepathing, providing the possibility of unlimited freedom of movement and exploration. The second difference was the ability to attribute information to elements in the landscape. These two characteristics were critical to the concept of designing and planning in an information-rich environment.

Until recently, neither the physical nor the digital visual simulations were portable; both required the stakeholders to travel to the production location. In addition, they were expensive to use in the context of planning and design, in terms of initial cost, and the time and effort needed to construct the 3D models in either digital or physical format.

The advent of increasingly powerful personal computers equipped with sophisticated graphics software and hardware dramatically reduced the initial cost and complexity of 3D real-time visual simulations. More recently, powerful laptops and lightweight projectors have made it possible to take the simulations to the stakeholders rather than requiring that they come to the lab (figure 1.18). Portability has substantively changed the ability to integrate real-time 3D visual simulation more fully with public participation, opening up new possibilities for collaborative decision making.

PDDSS take advantage of 2D and 3D visualization and analysis technologies to combine them in a powerful decision-support environment. Two-dimensional mapping and analytical software GIS are linked with 3D interactive simulation

Figure 1.18 – 3D simulations that once required large, expensive gantry-mounted cameras and/or computers can now be realized on inexpensive portable laptops with projectors, allowing planners to bring interactive 3D to workshop participants. (Houston Near Northside Economic Revitalization Plan). (Environmental Simulation Center, 2001)

Figure 1.19 – In conjunction with the Kona Community Development Plan "How Do We Grow?" workshop, CommunityViz™ was used to support stakeholder exploration of alternative development scenarios in both a 2D GIS map and a 3D real-time model, making changes and evaluating impacts on the fly. (Environmental Simulation Center, 2006)

software, to allow users to think, design, analyze, and experience place in both 2D and 3D for a more holistic approach to planning. In addition, the fourth dimension of time can be designed into the representation for public participation and decision-making processes. This allows the user to forecast the impacts of public and private decisions and develop scenarios in both 2D and virtual reality 3D (such as in CommunityViz™ and ESRI's ArcScene). It is now possible to analyze the scenarios' results on the fly, and refine the alternative scenarios in a nonlinear, nonhierarchical fashion in both 2D and 3D. In CommunityViz™, the three-dimensional representation of alternatives in an information-rich interactive virtual reality environment transcends the use of visualization as merely illustration (figure 1.19).

SUMMARY

The simultaneous coming of age of the two fields that make up the narrative of this book—public involvement and digital visualization—and the increased flexibility and sophistication of available tools are profoundly changing the way decisions about planning issues are made. First, the process of decision making is becoming increasingly transparent, with the public becoming involved early in the process. Second, the ability to visualize alternatives and understand their impact has made public choices increasingly better informed. Finally, the use of computers and GIS-linked 3D imagery has dramatically shortened the time needed for feedback. While at one time it took several meetings to enable the public to make decisions, today feedback occurs instantaneously, enabling the same group of people to test alternatives and make informed decisions within a single meeting.

The technology is continuing to change. For example, Google Earth™ has begun to make the use of real-time visual simulation both more affordable and accessible to the public. Provided free over the Internet, users of the 3D Google Earth™ can now construct and add their own 3D models of buildings to a growing shared library that can then be used in a planning process and disseminated via the Internet. The construction of 3D environments has been simplified through the use of Google Earth's™ authoring tools (Google SketchUp™), and the cost of creating 3D environments has been drastically reduced.

2. Benefits, Principles, and Lessons Learned

Having gained a place at the planning decision-making table, the public is there to stay. Hardly a plan being developed today does not include various degrees of public involvement. Planning professionals, elected officials, and developers have learned that the costs of not involving the public at the outset of a project are high. On the other hand, digital visualization tools have only recently begun to find acceptance in planning. They are perceived as difficult to use, rapidly changing, and expensive to operate.

BENEFITS OF INTEGRATING VISUALIZATION TOOLS WITH PUBLIC INVOLVEMENT

The integration of digital visualizations has dramatically changed how a democratic public involvement process is structured. As these benefits become better known and the costs of software, hardware, and labor diminish, the use of visualizations will increase. This will result in rigorous attention to the use and integration of visualizations with the public process. The benefits include:

- *Placing information at the public's fingertips*. Visualizations distill enormous data resources in ways that are intuitively understood by the public. Citizens have access to the same information as planners, and that enables them to make sound, informed decisions (figure 2.1).

- *Test driving the future*. Whether illustrating transportation or land use alternatives (or both), visual simulations clarify planning options. The public is given clear choices and can better define what course of action is best for the community (figure 2.2).

- *Securing instant feedback*. Visualizations close the "response gap" on projects by providing instantaneous feedback on fundamental decisions. In a four-hour workshop, the public can create and refine proposals and review them within seconds of changes being made (figure 2.3).

- *Gaining permission to act*. The public process encourages communities to develop a shared vision. Visualizations communicate a clear image of where the community wants to go. Leaders can see the direction of public vision and can lead from there having gained permission to act (figure 2.4).

The BluePrint Houston Citizens Congress held in May 2003 was attended by 1,175 residents. They used electronic keypads to express their support of the goals and recommendations of the vision. (ACP–Visioning & Planning)

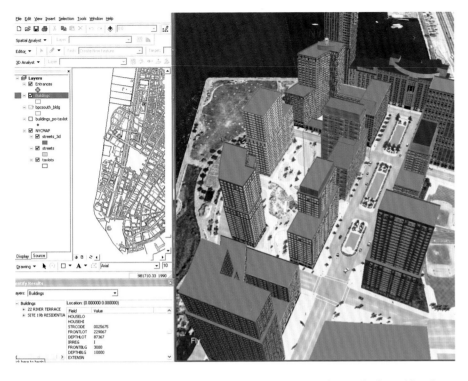

Figure 2.1 – In this 3D GIS of Battery Park City's north neighborhood in New York City, a database with zoning, building, and site information is linked to a real-time 3D model. The image shows a build-out of the neighborhood under one of many zoning and building massing alternatives. (Environmental Simulation Center, 2001)

Figure 2.2 – Examples of images used in a "How Do We Grow?" workshop in Houston: 3D visualization shows a commercial corridor with the typical scenario of parking in front (above) and an alternative scenario where parking is relocated to the rear and replaced by a cafe (below). (Houston Near Northside Economic Revitalization Plan; Environmental Simulation Center, 2001)

PRACTICAL PRINCIPLES

The specifics of public involvement techniques are described in the next chapter, but a number of practical principles have been identified to guide the design of public involvement processes that avail themselves of digital visualizations.

Designing a Democratic Public Process

Several principles serve as the foundation for designing a successful public involvement process and provide a vehicle for the introduction of digital visualizations.

- *Inclusiveness*. Inclusiveness is what lends lasting legitimacy and power to a democratic public process. In designing a process, no opportunity should be overlooked to ensure that the mix of participants reflects the diversity of the community in which the process is taking place. Inclusiveness requires the implementation of specific outreach efforts targeted to demographic and special interest groups, as well as efforts to ensure that participants come from diverse geographical areas (i.e., the inner city, specific neighborhoods, suburbia, and exurbia).

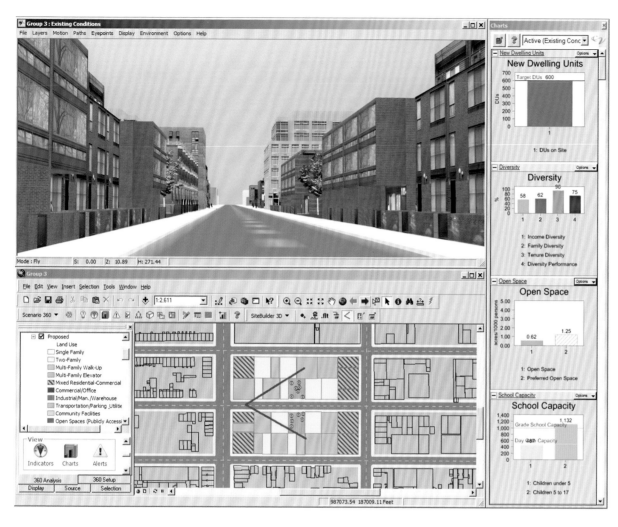

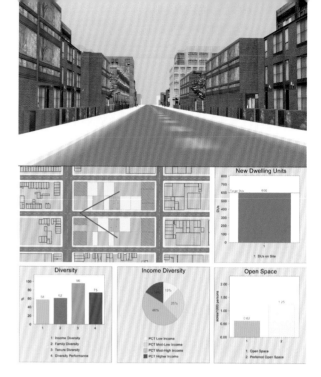

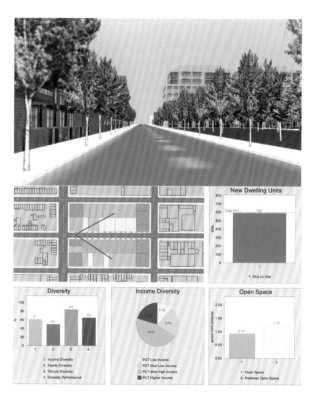

Figure 2.3 – Using 3D GIS for iterative design at a Lincoln Institute Visioning and Visualization Workshop. The image above shows the working interface of CommunityViz™ and the area map with a locator view cone and legend on the lower left, the 3D view above, and various performance indicators on the right. The initial design produced by a team of workshop participants and its performance indicators is shown on the upper right. The team members decided that they needed more green space in their design and, through an iterative process, they began moving and eliminating buildings to create a large park on the south side of the street, and added street trees. As they eliminated smaller scale townhouses to enlarge the open space (lower right), the benchmark for the total number of units fell significantly below the target. To compensate, they substituted larger buildings with more units on another part of the site. This, in turn, improved income diversity on the site, but lowered family and tenure diversity. This type of real-time feedback informs the design process and frames the choices and trade-offs that must be made. (Environmental Simulation Center, 2005)

Figure 2.4 – An aerial view of a 3D real-time model of a proposed Growth Opportunity Area (GOA) that emerged during the Kona Community Development Plan "Where Do We Grow?" workshop. The GOA was constructed by assembling "Kona building blocks" in a pattern that reflects the kind of compact mixed-use development and density the community favored. (Environmental Simulation Center, 2006)

- *Practicality*. A public process must contain the seeds that will enable the implementation of its outcomes. To achieve that, participants should be able to see, understand, and test the environmental, spatial, economic, political, and social implications of what has been proposed. The process has to be designed as a two-way learning experience in which the intuitive knowledge of residents blends with technical data.

- *Creativity*. This objective is achieved in the way participants interact with one another. A meeting design that is too rigid, does not allow for growth and learning, and is dominated by the few will constrain the creativity and potentiality of participants. Conversely, a meeting design that is based on fair, agreed-upon rules, rich in information, safe, and interactive will encourage the growth and expansion of creativity.

Robert Dahl, Sterling Professor Emeritus of Political Science at Yale University, has suggested that in a democracy the process for making binding decisions has at least two distinguishable stages: "setting the agenda and deciding the outcome . . . [where] setting the agenda is the part of the process during which matters are selected on which decisions are to be made . . . [and] deciding the outcome, or the decisive stage, is the period during which the process culminates in an outcome." Dahl (1989) outlines some criteria for a democratic process:

- *Transparency*. By definition, a democratic public process requires transparency, which is achieved by structuring the process along a clearly defined path that links deliberations and enables participants to make all critical decisions in the open through face-to-face discussions, collaboration, and accommodation.

- *Comprehensiveness*. The process should cut across the boundaries of specialized professional disciplines and enable participants to connect the dots and explore solutions across a variety of topics. To achieve the necessary degree of comprehensiveness, participants need to be given the tools to envision a true-to-life, complex, all-inclusive snapshot of their community and of the issues having an impact on the plan.

- *Effective participation*. Citizens should have adequate opportunity for effective participation, including placing questions on the agenda that are to be decided during the democratic process. All participation should be inclusive.

- *Voting equality*. At the decisive stage, each citizen must have an equal opportunity to express a choice that is equal in weight to the choices of others.

- *Enlightened understanding*. This assumes each individual has adequate and equal opportunity to access information and to come to their own conclusions.

Choosing the Appropriate Tools

Information technology, and particularly digital visual simulation, can be extremely seductive. Before one begins to select tools, one should consider what should and should not be done to help structure the selection and evaluation of tools and their integration in the process.

- *Place-based tools.* Tools must be able to be localized. Tools must accommodate the values and preferences of the community by supporting the community's formulation of performance criteria or indicators to be used to evaluate community-generated planning and design alternatives. Tools that are shells that need to be filled by the community, rather than those that are preprogrammed, can facilitate an open, democratic participatory process, while those with built-in values or defaults may represent a trade-off between ease of use and community-defined specificity.

- *Precision and accuracy.* Precision should not be confused with accuracy. Computers are notoriously precise, but not necessarily accurate. For example, in the architectural and engineering CAD world, dimensions can be calculated to the twentieth decimal place. Whether the dimensions and enclosing angles are accurate is another matter. Vision plans and planning, urban design policy, and decision making tend not to need a high level of either precision or accuracy, within acceptable tolerances, in part because the types of decisions being made are broad and the legal standard for information used to make the decision is less demanding (e.g., developing a vision plan versus project review). Further, as in the real world, much of the information in the GIS database will have varying levels of precision and accuracy as well as data freshness.

- *Calibrating information and managing project resources.* The soft underbelly of most digital planning tools is the database. A good way to approach the creation of an easy-to-use, understandable database, whether in two or three dimensions, involves two interlocking principles: (1) need to know, and (2) how close is good enough? Building the spatial database on a need-to-know basis—by focusing on the data layers and 3D models critical to informing the questions asked or the decisions to be made—recognizes that data/information is not only often difficult and expensive to create,

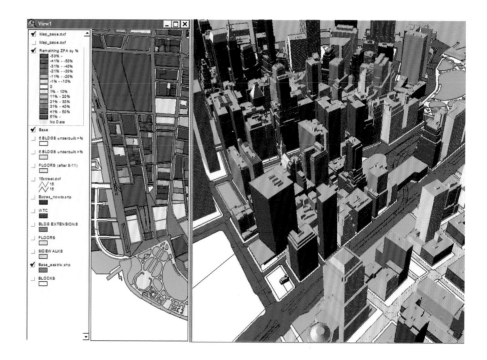

Figure 2.5 – The Environmental Simulation Center's 3D GIS of Lower Manhattan was used to develop the Greenwich Street South Urban Design Plan. This example illustrates the analytical and visual capacities of 3D GIS to represent in three dimensions and in tables which buildings are either overbuilt (in red) or underbuilt (in blue) per the city's zoning resolution. As buildings are constructed, they are added to the database and 3D massing model. The same 3D models can be reused and colored differently to visualize and assess zoning alternatives, augmented as buildings are built, and photo-textured for pedestrian-level real-time walk-throughs. (Environmental Simulation Center, 2004)

but equally difficult and expensive to maintain and update (figure 2.5). The approach assumes that the 2D/3D database is always a work in progress, is never finished, and therefore is never perfect.

The best digital tools are those that allow one to enrich the database continuously without discarding the original and starting over again (figure 2.6). The question, how close is good enough?, addresses the level of precision and accuracy required to inform citizens' choices. Typically, as accuracy increases so do the costs, raising a cost-benefit question as to whether the added increment of information adds substantially to the quality of the deliberative process and is the best allocation of resources.

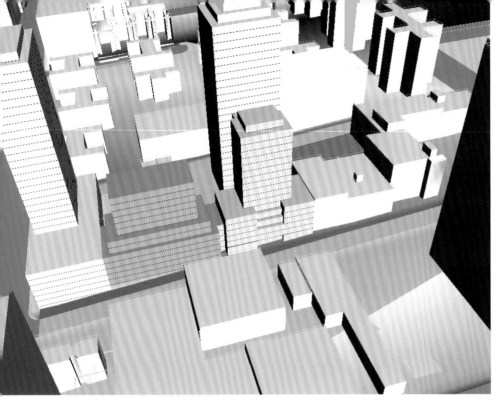

Figure 2.6 – The 3D massing model (above left) and the photorealistic textured model (above right) were both used in real time at the public hearing before the New York City Planning Commission and therefore had to be dimensionally and visually accurate. The image on the lower right shows the actual project under construction in Manhattan's Lincoln Square district. (Environmental Simulation Center, 2002–2008)

LESSONS LEARNED

When choosing visualization tools, several lessons need to be considered:

Lesson one: *Tools are enablers.*

Integrating tools and public process is about more than identifying tools that will enhance current practice. In many instances the technology makes it possible to do things that could not have been done before (or only at a great cost), which, as a result, influences the design of the process itself.

Lesson two: *Be creative with software and tools.*

The names of software and tools appropriate to the situation at hand may not include the words *planning* or *urban design* because these tools can range from the generic to the specific, and the functions they can perform in one area can be applied to another.

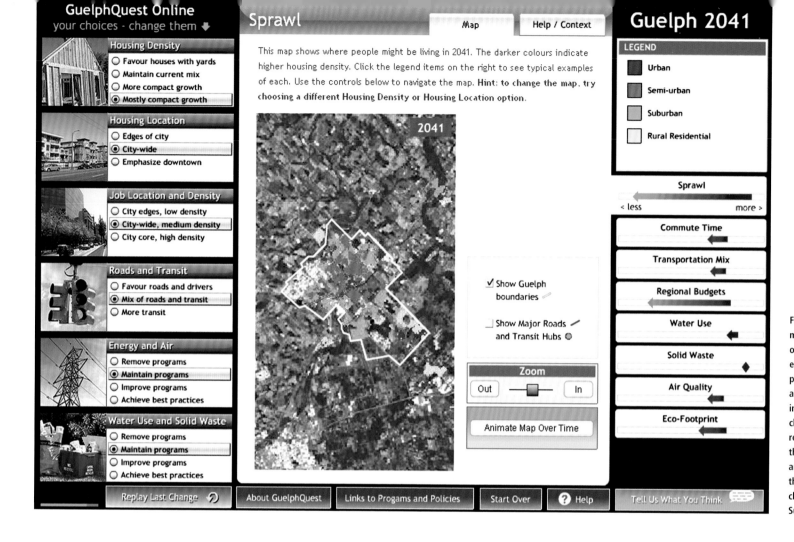

Figure 2.7 – The MetroQuest™ model of future growth in the City of Guelph, Ontario, was created to educate and involve citizens in the planning of the region. It has an attractive, interactive Web-based interface that prompts users to make choices for the future, quantifies the results of those choices, and allows the users to change their choices and see how those changes impact the results relative to their original choices. (Courtesy of Envision Sustainability Tools, Inc.)

An example of a generic tool is GIS, which can be used for land planning and visioning, epidemiological studies, disaster management, political districting, business, and other work. Because it is a generic tool, users will develop their own applications and, where needed, their own scripts or commands, which are often shared online with other users. While GIS is not quite open source, where a user has full access to the code (such as Linux, an open system that treats the user or contributor as a resource rather than a customer), the limited access does allow for customization and fine tuning to a specific application. Most PDDSS tools and software (e.g., CommunityViz™ and INDEX) fall into this category.

It is important to be clear about one's needs, as this will inform one's choice of tool. Real-time virtual reality 3D software deployed in CommunityViz™, for example, came from military and industrial applications where the objects in the landscape could have information attributed to them that could be queried or quantified, such as, in the case of a residential building, the predominant use of the building, its age, height, floor area, zoning designation, number of dwelling units, and dwelling units per acre.

Lesson three: *Not all tools are adaptable.*
Many tools have been designed for specific applications and may not be adaptable to situations other than those for which they were conceived (figure 2.7). Traffic, air- and water-quality models and software, and some planning software are prepackaged and can be localized only to the extent that they deal

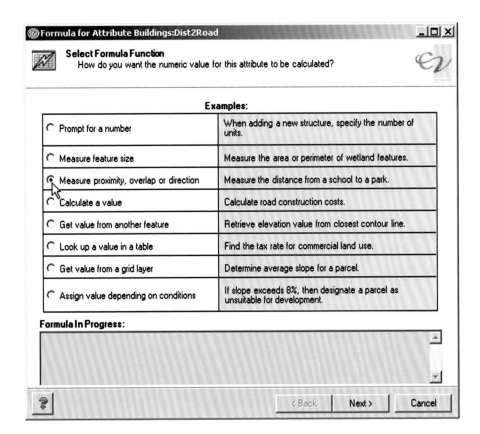

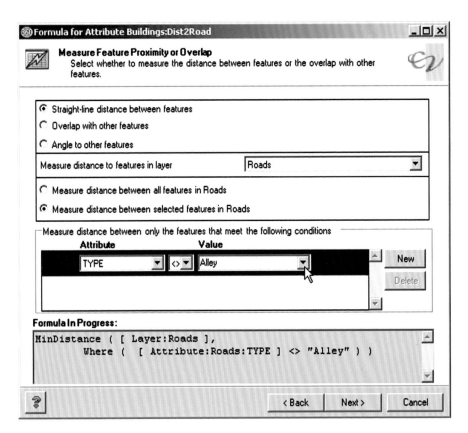

Figure 2.8 – CommunityViz's™ Scenario 360 has many "wizards" that help create basic formulas and indicators as well as more complex site-suitability or build-out models. In this three-part example, the wizard guides the user through creating a formula to calculate the distance between buildings and roads. Specifically, the wizard first asks the user what to do. In this case, the user selects "Measure proximity, overlap, or direction."

In the second screen, the wizard prompts the user for the GIS layer containing the features the user wants to measure the distance to—in this case, "Roads." However, the user may want to exclude any distances to alleys, so the user can select the option to "Measure distance between selected features in Roads." The user specifies that the only type of roads they want to measure to are not alleys (Attribute: TYPE <> Value: Alley).

with locally generated data. Because they are prepackaged and rarely open source, this type of software, model, or tool tends to be a "black box," where the operations, standards, and defaults are rarely transparent and need to be fully and clearly explained to gain the confidence of the participants in an open democratic process.

Lesson four: *Know your terminology.*
In selecting tools one should be aware of the difference among models, software, and applications. Digital models are not 3D models of buildings and the landscape, but rather comprise a program or series of integrated programs

that perform a task. Typically, models do not have the graphical user interface (GUI, pronounced "gooey") found in commercial software and require a high level of user expertise and technical documentation. Out-of-the-box software, on the other hand, is ready to use, fully documented, supported by a help desk, with a fully developed GUI and "wizards" that, for example, help a user formulate impact or performance indicators by prompting the user step by step (figure 2.8). Applications are developed on top of generic software. Writing applications will often require that the user have a higher level of expertise, including an understanding of how the software on which the application sits functions.

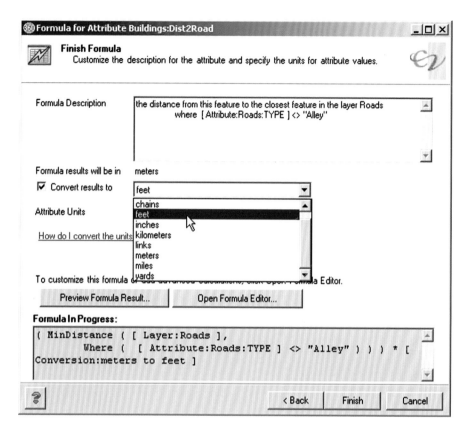

Finally, the user wants the measurement to be in feet so he selects "Convert results to: feet." As the user selects these options in plain English, the formula is automatically written in the correct Visual Basic syntax and displayed in the bottom window of the wizard. (Environmental Simulation Center, 2008)

Lesson five: *Try it before buying it.*

Software should be tested before being selected and purchased. A demonstration copy of the software or model enables a process designer to test it using localized community data. Too often sales and marketing descriptions create expectations that may overstate the functionality of the software when it is used in practice.

Lesson six: *Be clear about what you want to do.*

Most applications in visioning, planning, and urban design require the use of more than one software package. Depending on the application and the software packages being used, this can become a frustrating task, although

interoperability between software packages has and will continue to improve. To help in the evaluation of software options, the user should develop a narrative or functional specification that describes what the application is meant to do (e.g., the type of public process to be used, its setting, and the characteristics and number of people involved, questions that need to be answered, and issues to be addressed).

SUMMARY

The benefits, principles, and lessons presented in this chapter provide a framework for the more specific examinations of public involvement techniques and visual simulation tools that follow. Collectively, these can be used as a "punch list" to integrate the design of a public process with the selection of appropriate digital tools.

When organized in an open and transparent way, and following rigorous criteria in the selection of visual simulation tools, the public process becomes an effective tool for democratic decision making and consensus building. These democratic processes result in a consistency for change that, in turn, saves time and money, minimizes dissent, creates a positive investment climate, and provides an incentive to elected officials to make tough decisions with an understanding that agreement is in place to support those decisions.

3. Public Involvement Techniques in Planning

Public involvement techniques and visualization tools are widely available today to engage the public and facilitate informed planning and design decision making. Together these powerful techniques and tools are reshaping the practice of planning and creating better neighborhoods, cities, and regions in which to live.

An emphasis on public involvement begs the questions, what is the role of technical information in a public-driven planning process, and what are the roles of staff, consultants, and experts? Giving a voice to the public in the initial stages of a plan does not imply that the role of the experts diminishes. To the contrary, as the dialog with the public is established, the role played by consultants, staff, and experts grows. In practical terms a public process requires higher standards of performance and involvement on the part of the expert.

The use of information-rich, GIS-based visualization technology facilitates the exchange of information in a visual and nonthreatening environment. The public benefits from the data, which enables them to make informed decisions, and the professional gains priceless insights on what works in a community and what does not. The result is a process in which all players learn from each other in addition to contributing insights and ideas.

This chapter focuses on visions and charrettes, two types of public involvement activities that have gained recognition and acceptance in the planning field and have proven to be effective vehicles for the integration of visualization tools in communities.

VISIONS AND CHARRETTES

Visions are inclusive and comprehensive public involvement programs designed to anticipate, visualize, measure, and plan the future of a neighborhood, city, or region. Visions have been used extensively at the regional scale, as they often are the only way to reach agreement in complex multijurisdictional conditions. In the twenty years following Vision 2000 in Chattanooga, Tennessee, visions have undergone profound transformations while remaining true to the basic principles of inclusiveness, transparency, careful design, and commitment to implementation.

The participants in this Champaign, Illinois, visioning workshop list factors that make strong places strong and weak places weak. The lessons learned in the workshop were then used to identify remedies. (ACP–Visioning & Planning)

Figure 3.1 – During a New York World Trade Center charrette workshop, participants draw concepts and sketch ideas. (ACP–Visioning & Planning)

There are three distinctive outcomes to a vision:

1. The values, which represent what residents genuinely want;

2. The vision, which articulates the way the community can address those values; and

3. The policies, which determine how the vision can be implemented.

To arrive at those outcomes, participants follow a sequence of steps that include brainstorming and envisioning the future, organizing ideas generated through the brainstorming, and developing goals and strategies supported by those ideas. Visions can deal with all areas of interest to a community in an unconstrained manner or can focus on specific planning issues such as the establishment of the policy foundation of a comprehensive plan. A vision process typically lasts from six to eight months and produces an agreed-upon and articulated vision for a preferred future with recommendations on how that future can be realized.

Charrettes are concentrated, multidisciplinary planning or design activities characterized by an intense period of work and periodic reviews of the products of that work with the public. Charrettes typically deal with smaller areas of a community than visions, for example, a downtown, a redevelopment area, or a neighborhood. When dealing with larger areas, several coordinated and sometimes simultaneous charrettes may take place. An example is the twenty-five design and planning charrettes organized as part of the Imagine New York process in the New York City metropolitan area in the aftermath of the terrorist attacks on the World Trade Center of September 11, 2001 (figure 3.1).

In a short period of time, typically a week, a charrette can produce highly developed design alternatives and plans with citizen buy-in. During the public involvement part of a charrette, citizens and stakeholders work as a team with designers and planners, and use maps and drawings to develop design alternatives for a given physical area of a community. As key areas of agreement are identified, they become the focus for further refinement. When preparation and follow-up periods are included, charrettes take three to four months to complete.

Both visions and charrettes are effective for gaining public input into physical plans. They are not mutually exclusive and are often used together. Visions, in fact, often establish the planning context within which charrettes can be conducted.

PREPARATORY STEPS

Both visions and charrettes require careful preparation and rigorous structuring of their processes. Preparation starts with the creation of a leadership team to assist in the design of the process itself and in the development of an outreach campaign to attract participation.

Assembling a Leadership Team

A public involvement activity may be initiated by one of three entities. A government may require it as part of a planning or redevelopment project; private developers may want to have the public input on their specific project; or, civic leaders may want to set a consensus agenda to guide private investments and public decisions. Regardless of who initiates a public process, it is critical to form a leadership team to guide and lend credibility to it.

A leadership team contributes to the success of a public involvement initiative in subtle ways. From the perspective of the government, the creation of a leadership team lends transparency to the planning process. From the point of view of the private developer, the leadership team brings to the table a balanced interlocutor. From the standpoint of civic leaders, the leadership team represents a first step in expanding the circle of participation.

The leadership team becomes the public face of a vision or charrette. It reassures residents to the extent that it reflects the diversity of the community in its composition. It bridges the gap between the initiators or developers of a project and residents. It invites and energizes the community to participate and sets the tone for that participation. By maintaining the integrity of the public process, it represents the interests of the broader community. It engenders good will and often becomes an incubator for future community stewards and leaders.

A leadership team's members must credibly reflect the perspectives and experiences of the broader community. Any large group from the community ought to be able to identify with at least one member of the team. Some of the members should be or have been responsible for the community, both officially (e.g., past and present elected or appointed leaders) and unofficially (such as advocates for projects and initiatives). They have exercised power in a fair and responsible way. Other members should be balanced and neutral individuals, whose participation is not influenced by an association with any key interests. Strong facilitative leaders whose primary focus is on promoting and sustaining the collaborative process rather than on advocating a particular point of view also should be included.

The leadership team must be a constituency for change. That is, it must collectively possess the influence to hold established authorities and implementing organizations accountable for implementation of its recommendations. It should commit to steer the process and should also be prepared to champion the implementation of the recommendations once agreement is reached. As such, the leadership team will steer the process from the very early steps to its end.

A leadership team can be appointed by a government entity, created informally through early discussions between a developer and the community directly affected by a project, or convened by the civic leaders initiating a process. One of the first acts of a leadership team is to help design the process itself. Once that is accomplished the focus of the leadership team shifts to ensuring diverse participation.

Asking the Right Questions

The key to a successful public involvement process rests in the type of questions asked of the participants. What question is asked, when it is asked, and how it is asked are critical to the success of a program and the quality of its outcome. The questions will define the type and character of the public involvement process and its outcomes.

As explained in chapter 1, the conventional way to approach the public starts with the wrong question: How do you like this proposal? (figure 3.2). This question also is typically raised in the wrong setting—the public hearing, which is often conducted in an intimidating assembly-like setting. The question is also raised at the wrong time, after experts have deliberated and when the plan is near completion, turning the participants' comments into mere footnotes to the process. Reliance on this type of meeting has given public involvement an aura

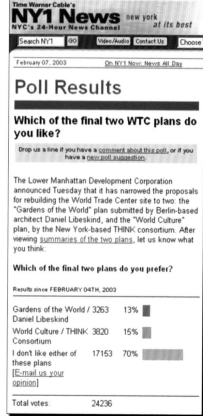

Figure 3.2 – The Lower Manhattan Development Corporation picked two final plans and asked the public what they thought about each one. As shown by this informal Web poll, most people did not like either of the plans. (Courtesy of NY1 News, a Division of Time Warner Cable LLC)

of futility and created public distrust. Most public hearings, according to Daniel Kemmis (1990), have become "public screamings," in which the protagonists do not listen to each other's arguments.

Visions and charrettes start by asking a very different question: What do we want? They follow that question with other questions designed to understand and refine what the public wants. In a vision, the question structures the brainstorming phase of the process. In a charrette, the question is addressed through mapping activities and expressed through drawings. The question is always asked at the very beginning of the process, before a plan is developed, giving value to the participants' comments. The setting of the question is typically within the structure of facilitated small groups, a safe environment calibrated to enhance creativity and release imaginative thinking.

DESIGNING A PUBLIC INVOLVEMENT PROCESS

In the design of a democratic public involvement process, one size will not fit all. One of the first activities of a leadership team is to define the objectives (the desired outcomes) of the process and then work with staff and consultants to review what available tools and techniques best fit these objectives.

A rich toolbox of meeting techniques is available to conduct visions and charrettes. Those described in this chapter best allow for the integration of visualization tools. It is by no means a complete list. They are organized into three groups: generative techniques used to gather ideas from the public; analytical techniques used to refine outcomes and address critical questions; and deliberative techniques used to prioritize results and give closure to the process. These three sets of techniques represent steps that almost any public involvement process needs to follow.

Generative Techniques

Public visions and charrettes have the purpose of gathering ideas, measuring the public's responses to visuals, and gauging the public's understanding of and response to specific issues.

Idea Gathering   Gathering ideas from the public is the first and most important step of any public process. This is where the question, what do we want?, is first raised. During a vision, in meetings that take place in various parts of a community,

Figure 3.3 – Multilingual facilitation at public meetings is used to attract those who are less likely to participate due to language barriers. (ACP–Visioning & Planning)

residents are asked to envision the community's potential. The ideas are carefully recorded so that no single idea is lost. Trained facilitators ensure that the process occurs in a safe environment conducive to creative and productive thinking. Participants learn to interact with each other to identify things they treasure, things they want to preserve, and things they would like to re-create (if lost). In doing so they imagine a desired future for their community (figure 3.3).

In a charrette, participants brainstorm on a map using pens and pencils to draw ideas or, in the emerging field of electronic charrettes, they use laptop computers. At the end of this type of meeting, participants present their ideas and drawings in a pin-up period. The presentations show the areas where clear agreement is emerging and where more work needs to be done. The results become the springboard for the development of alternatives or the refinement of plans.

Strong Places, Weak Places   This technique is a variation on the well-established SWOT (strengths, weaknesses, opportunities, and threats) procedure. Strong Places, Weak Places uses a map of the planning areas and asks participants to identify specific locations on the map that represent strong and weak places. The identification of strong places leads to an understanding of the physical qualities that make those places strong in the mind of residents. The identification of weak places leads to an exploration of why those places are seen as weak. In many cases, the lessons learned from what makes strong places strong can be used in addressing the issues identified with the weak places. This technique is very useful in the early stages of a vision plan or charrette because it enables the gathering of ideas linked directly to the physical reality of a community (figure 3.4).

Figure 3.4 – The Strong Places, Weak Places exercise is used during a charrette workshop in Ada Township, Michigan, to bring attention to problem areas and to illustrate physical conditions that work well in a community. (ACP–Visioning & Planning)

Figure 3.5 – For the Houston Near Northside Economic Revitalization Plan, an "apples-to-apples" 3D visualization was created to compare two scenarios for a pedestrian-oriented neighborhood commercial corridor: parking in front (above) and parking in rear (below). (Environmental Simulation Center, 2000)

Visual Surveys Visualizations in the form of visual surveys can be used in an idea-gathering meeting. A visual survey technique emphasizes measuring participants' preferences. The surveys use photographs, computer-generated graphics, and real-time 3D models as tools to trigger participants' responses. They work extremely well in gauging the public's preferences in order to develop design guidelines or to identify preferred development scenarios.

In Vision 2030, in the Baltimore region, visual surveys were used to identify the public's preference for alternative yet equivalent development patterns in terms of households. The patterns were illustrated using 3D bird's-eye-view models. For the Kona, Hawaii, Community Development Plan, visual simulations were used to illustrate how diverse densities could be integrated in the creation of proposed villages and to measure the public's support of the mixed-use, mixed-density villages. In Houston's Near Northside Economic Revitalization Plan, 3D images derived from a real-time 3D model were used both to illustrate alternating development patterns and identify the public's preferences (figure 3.5).

Figure 3.6 – More than 400 Kona residents involved with the Kona Community Development Plan participated in the Mapping the Future workshop. (ACP–Visioning & Planning)

Figure 3.7 – At the end of a charrette workshop, each small group reports its findings and recommendations to the whole assembly. (ACP–Visioning & Planning)

Critical Questions   In a critical-question technique, participants working in small groups can address specific questions on issues that emerge as critical in the development of a plan. Different small groups can address individual questions. A sharing of responses in assembly follows the small-group deliberations. The totality of the responses provides a vivid picture of the depth of understanding of the issues as well as revealing emerging agreements. For example in Kona, Hawaii, the critical-questions technique was used to measure the degree of public support for growth and development (figure 3.6). It was also used to gain an understanding of how to address and treat the wealth of ancestral sites, which are of great importance to the native Hawaiian population and can be found throughout the planning area.

Analytical Techniques

Deduction is a form of reasoning in which a conclusion is derived from something known (such as a database of ideas or factual information). When applied to a vision or charrette, the analytical process might involve reviewing a body of ideas gathered through brainstorming meetings, or querying a database such as a GIS, either in two or three dimensions. A question or sequence of questions can organize information in order to make better sense of the possible implications of the data when looked at in combination with other layers of data or fields.

In public involvement meetings that use analytical techniques, participants are asked to analyze information and draw conclusions. While the generative meetings elicit a more intuitive response from the participants, analytical meetings require an intense interaction between the public and the data. At these meetings data-rich visualization tools such as Index™ or CommunityViz™ find extensive applications.

Drafting Policies   After gathering ideas, drafting policies is the second critical step in a vision. All ideas collected are put into a database in which they are organized into topical categories that provide a first glance at the depth and breadth of the public vision. They need, however, to be analyzed, interpreted, and drafted as policies and concrete strategies. In a vision, the drafting of policies and strategies takes place in public meetings organized around individual categories of ideas. The outcome is policies that reflect the ideas and expectations of the community as well as a preliminary indication of the steps necessary to implement them. In a charrette, policy drafting is replaced by the identification of clear planning and design alternatives and scenarios. The multidisciplinary team of charrette professionals elaborates those alternatives and scenarios and brings them back to the public for review (figure 3.7).

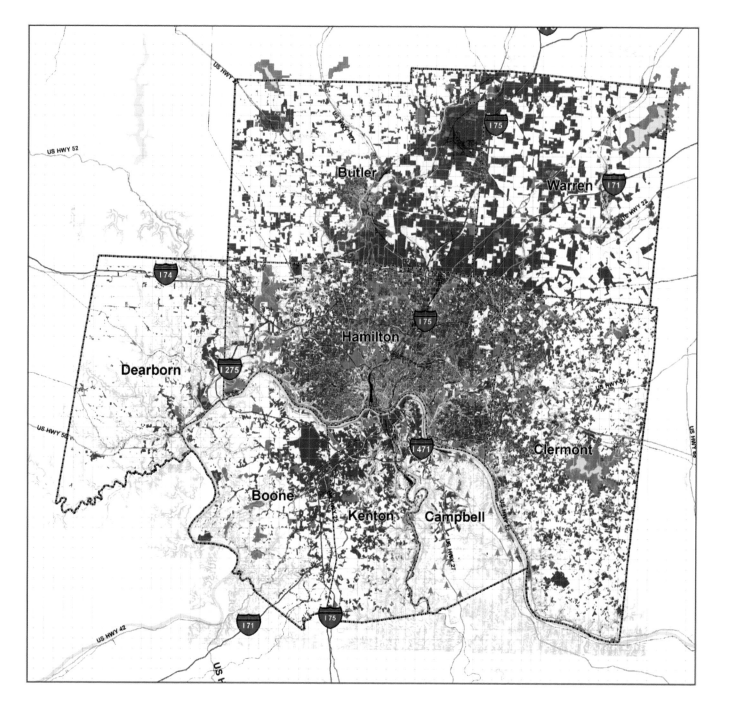

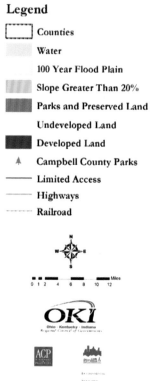

The OKI Region

Regional Workshop
June 10, 2002

Legend

	Counties
	Water
	100 Year Flood Plain
	Slope Greater Than 20%
	Parks and Preserved Land
	Undeveloped Land
	Developed Land
⚐	Campbell County Parks
—	Limited Access
—	Highways
⋯	Railroad

Figure 3.8 – A Where Do We Grow? generalized land use and constraint map used in a regional workshop for the Ohio, Kentucky, and Indiana Regional Council of Governments. The map shows developed land in gray, parks and protected land in green, and land constrained by steep slopes in pink. (Environmental Simulation Center, 2002)

Understanding Growth   The technique known as Reality Check is widely used in regional visions to further an understanding of physical growth and development in the region and the trade-offs that come with it. The Where Do We Grow? workshop guides participants in exploring future growth options based on development trends and population and employment forecasts (see Baltimore case study in chapter 6). The activity works best at the regional scale and in areas where the expected growth is strong. Participants use generalized land use maps that indicate developed areas, areas already protected from development, any environmental constraints (for example, steep slopes), and major transportation infrastructure (figure 3.8).

Participants are first asked to identify and set aside land that should be protected from future development, forever or for a determined amount of time. In setting aside land, participants agree on criteria. For example, they can agree to protect land to create a natural growth boundary, or they can agree to use the protection of land as a way to create wildlife corridors.

After agreement is reached on land protection the focus shifts to accommodating future growth. Participants now place on the map adhesive chips that represent the land needed to accommodate future growth based on current land consumption trends (figure 3.9). In the course of the exercise, participants discuss preferred ways to accommodate future growth and locate it on the map. They can express a full range of options in accommodating future growth including continuing current trends, changing densities, and compacting development patterns, among others.

This type of exercise makes extensive use of GIS data. The results can be visualized by showing before and after images and live fly-bys that indicate recommended changes in densities and development patterns. The results can also be quantified by translating the information provided by each small group into a composite map (figure 3.10). The information derived from the Where Do We Grow? workshop leads to the development of scenarios that are then explored further.

The Open House   The Open House is a key activity in the course of a charrette. It typically takes place midway in the charrette week and it offers the public an opportunity to interact with the interdisciplinary team while they are developing and refining aspects of the plan.

Figure 3.9 – During a Where Do We Grow? workshop for Imagine Manatee, Manatee County, Florida, participants place on the map chips that represent the amount of land needed to accommodate projected population at current land use consumption trends. Participants can put chips on vacant land, stack them to indicate a desire for higher density, and put them on existing development, indicating a desire for infill and/or redevelopment. (ACP–Visioning & Planning)

When using visualization tools, the Open House is an opportunity to present solutions and to engage the public in evaluating those solutions using the tools' rich GIS-linked data. The quiet, studio atmosphere of the Open House is conducive both to a dialogue between the charrette team and the public and to the creative testing of ideas (figure 3.11).

Deliberative Techniques

Deliberative techniques involve bringing workshop results back to the public for deliberation and prioritization.

Educating and Ratifying   In a vision, policies and strategies need to be ratified by a larger segment of the community to lend final credibility to the outcomes. To accomplish that, all the policies and strategies of the vision—which, up to now, have been developed by small groups—need to be presented in their entirety to the community at large. This requires publicizing the results widely,

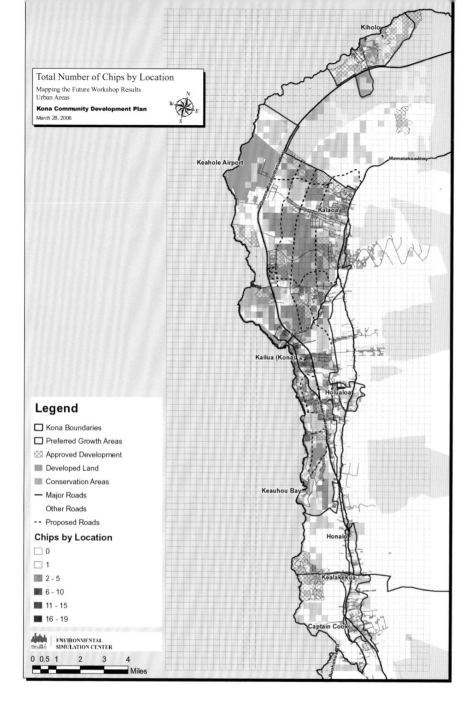

Legend

- ☐ Kona Boundaries
- ☐ Preferred Growth Areas
- ▨ Approved Development
- ▨ Developed Land
- ▨ Conservation Areas
- — Major Roads
-   Other Roads
- -- Proposed Roads

Chips by Location
- ☐ 0
- ☐ 1
- ▨ 2 - 5
- ▨ 6 - 10
- ▨ 11 - 15
- ▨ 16 - 19

Figure 3.10 – At the conclusion of the Kona Community Development Plan public workshop, each table's chip placement was entered into a GIS database. The resultant map showed areas where there was significant consensus for growth (the pink, purple, and dark blue areas, which represent the concentration of chips and level of consensus). (Environmental Simulation Center, 2006)

Figure 3.11 – This Open House in Fort Wayne, Indiana, offered a moment of reflection in the otherwise intense atmosphere of a charrette. (ACP–Visioning & Planning)

often working with local print and electronic media. Newspapers, for example, have helped distribute carefully designed inserts that provide information on the vision's outcomes and can also be used as surveys.

The public can also be brought together a final time to discuss the results, and to rate and rank individual proposals in priority order. To be credible, this type of final meeting needs to attract extensive participation, which requires considerable logistic coordination and the use of wireless technology (e.g., laptops and keypads) to quantify the public's responses (figure 3.12).

Random Telephone Surveys This powerful tool is used to test and verify with scientific certitude the outcomes of a process. Sampling size and duration of the survey are functions of the size of the community and budget. Surveys are best conducted toward the end of a process, and should be used to test outcomes that seem less certain. Surveys are particularly valuable in multijurisdictional situations, where elected officials may benefit most from the knowledge that their constituencies support the outcomes of the public process.

Figure 3.12 – Electronic keypad technology enables a large group of participants to express their preferences. The results of each inquiry are available instantaneously. (ACP–Visioning & Planning)

Choosing a Preferred Future   In large, regional visions it is often necessary to conduct an extended workshop and in some cases a second charrette. After the first charrette has identified a preferred development scenario, that scenario is translated into specific development patterns. The purpose of the extended workshop or second charrette is to test the potential development patterns and how they perform in the regional context.

Sometimes called the How Do We Grow? workshop, this activity requires the development of real-life digital models that illustrate how, for example, a neighborhood, a town center, or an infill development looks and performs using agreed-upon indicators. The workshop is highly interactive and uses prototypical building blocks as it engages participants in a place-building activity. In a complex region it is very likely that different patterns need to be tested, ranging from rural to suburban to urban conditions. Different indicators might be used to better meet the values and character of different parts of a region (figure 3.13).

PROMOTING PARTICIPATION AND BUILDING LEGITIMACY

Expanding the circle of participants from the center out is the most delicate activity in any public involvement process. Balanced and representative participation lends credibility to the effort, gains the attention of elected officials, and ensures that the resulting agreements are broadly shared.

The enlargement of the circle of participants is best accomplished by involving local residents at the very beginning, through the creation of an outreach committee made up of residents representing various parts of the planning area. Committee responsibilities include developing an outreach plan and implementing it. The outreach committee can be a subset of the leadership team.

The outreach plan should outline specific tactics to approach and invite participation to the public process. These tactics should follow the general principle that residents of a community are more likely to participate when someone whom they know and trust invites them. The outreach plan should strive for these three objectives:

- *Geographic diversity*. Efforts focus on ensuring balanced participation from residents from all parts of an area, including rural, suburban, and city residents. For example, in the Birmingham, Alabama, twelve-county region, twelve separate outreach committees were created and led by local leaders who were knowledgeable about how to attract local residents to the Region 2020 vision.

- *Demographic diversity*. Efforts target specific demographic groups to ensure the broadest possible participation including that of residents less likely to get involved. These include non-English-speaking residents, minorities, and specific age groups such as seniors, youth, and the elusive 20–39 age group. These groups often require variations in the involvement process. Non-English-speaking groups and transient populations, for example, often prefer a small focus group format to participation in larger meetings. The involvement of young people is best obtained through special meetings organized through the school system.

- *Involvement of area-wide organizations*. This requires outreach to local organizations with areawide membership such as the League of Women Voters, chambers of commerce, and the Sierra Club, to name a few. These organizations have extensive channels of communication, such as newsletters and electronic mailings, to inform and solicit the participation of members.

Outreach also needs to be supported by a parallel publicity effort that uses written and electronic media to create general awareness of the process and educate the public about critical issues for discussion.

Conventional Development

1990-99 Trends in Region

• Households	1000
• Jobs	1092
• Residential Gross	604 Acres
• Institutional:	97 Acres
• Commercial:	49 Acres
• Total Area:	750 Acres

Mixed-use Development

• Households	1000
• Jobs	1092
• Residential Gross	155 Acres
• Institutional:	97 Acres
• Commercial:	24 Acres
• Total Area:	276 Acres

Figure 3.13 – Prototypical development patterns used in the second Baltimore 2030 workshop show where households and jobs were held constant and land consumption was the variable. (Environmental Simulation Center, 2002)

SUMMARY

The menu of preparatory steps and techniques to implement a public involvement process represents just the tip of the iceberg in terms of what is being implemented on a daily basis in cities and regions throughout the country. It represents a compilation of basic steps that are constantly evolving as techniques are modified to accommodate the physical conditions of a place or the objectives of an effort. The extent to which these techniques support the use of digital databases, simulations, and visualizations has only been hinted at thus far. The next two chapters explore in greater detail how specific visualization tools have been applied in various public involvement programs.

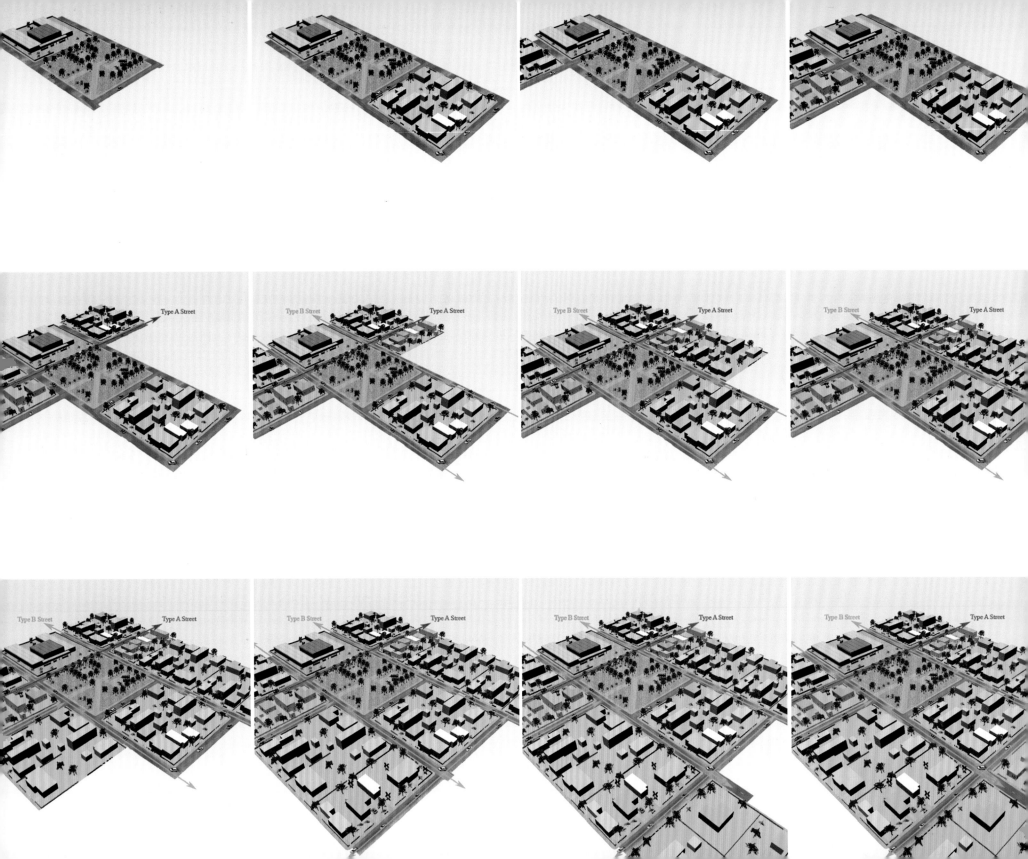

4. Visual Simulation Tools

Matching tools to a public participation process has become increasingly complicated. Tools are constantly being upgraded and new tools appear with regularity while others become obsolete or are no longer supported. This chapter focuses on an analysis of what is needed to accomplish specific tasks, rather than the details of a particularly attractive tool. Where specific tools are presented, the goal is to illustrate how they have been applied in a real-world situation. Examples of their application to projects jointly implemented by ACP–Visioning & Planning and the Environmental Simulation Center (ESC) demonstrate the correlation between desired outcomes and the selection of particular tools.

SELECTING THE APPROPRIATE TOOLS

The first step in developing a public involvement process that utilizes visual simulation tools is to match the tools with what the public or a client wants to accomplish. Once the task has been defined, the second step is to establish each tool's functionality and capacity, including their assets and liabilities. This section illustrates how a tool or set of tools can help to support a planning effort, for example a visioning process. In our experience it is rare for one digital tool to be responsive to all of a project's demands, hence the reference to a toolbox of various tools.

Toolbox Functionality

Digital tools should be able to communicate with each other, since different tools tend to function well at some scales and not others. This concept is often referred to as interoperability. The best tools are those that can help make a complex problem or set of issues sensible by providing the means to explain complexity rather than encourage oversimplification. Ideally, tools should be able to deal seamlessly with jumps in scale between local and regional actions to allow participants at a public meeting to better understand the effects of local actions on the region and vice versa.

Sample New Mexico–style 3D building blocks are assembled in a variety of ways to create a development scenario. (Environmental Simulation Center, Visioning and Visualization Workshop sponsored by the Lincoln Institute of Land Policy in Albuquerque, NM)

Tools should address the following functions:

- *Tools should be capable of integrating quantitative and qualitative issues.* Quantitative issues include infrastructure, the design of an urban corridor, and the presence or absence of sidewalks. Qualitative issues are more subjective, such as a "nice walk" (figure 4.1). Integrating the two requires tools that can assess the impacts of interrelated actions at the neighborhood, city, and regional scales, and evaluate the performance of the plan in the short, medium, and long terms.

- *Tools should support the formulation of performance indicators.* Performance indicators are used to evaluate how well an action, policy, or plan performs. They are often used along with benchmarks and capacities in impact analyses (e.g., what will happen at a given moment in time relative to the action(s) taken?). Unlike standards, such as the building envelope standards in form-based zoning, performance indicators frame the goal or objective to be achieved or the problem to be solved, and provide the tools to evaluate the performance of a policy, action, or plan. The best performance or impact analysis tools are those that allow for the community's customization to values and principles. While communities may opt to use the default performance indicators incorporated in the tool (e.g., minimum walking distance to a transit stop), the tools should also allow for the customization of performance indicators as well as the design and incorporation of new performance indicators.

- *Tools should be able to evaluate performance on the fly.* Tools should function well in community workshops where the participants may literally be building what-if scenarios of the future look and feel of their community (figure 4.2). Performance indicators in this context support dialog among the workshop participants by providing feedback on how well the scenarios perform against their own criteria and enabling scenarios to be refined in an iterative learning process.

- *Tools should be able to promote the identification of design options.* This may be as simple as static photomontages that illustrate what the design choices are, or as intuitive and interactive as a tool that encourages the user to try what-ifs, by building an environment in two and three dimensions.

- *Tools should be able to simulate design choices visually, whether in static 2D/3D or dynamic virtual reality 3D.* This is critical because the physical design of a place is translated into policy that will be experienced in the real world. It is an excellent way to test alternatives by comparing the design of a neighborhood, district, city, or region with policy statements and performance indicators that articulate the principles in quantitative and qualitative terms.

Tool Capacity

Tool capacity refers to the tool's accessibility, adaptability, affordability, and data requirements as well as its stability, ability to be updated, and maintenance.

- *Accessibility refers to local capacity to use the tool(s) on an ongoing basis rather than episodically.* It allows users to track change over time and continually evaluate both the performance of the vision plan and the resulting real world actions. Tools with very high learning curves may go unused, undermining the effort to build local capacity and transform the local institutional culture. Many operations will require talented professionals well into the future, but the community goal should be to use tools that are both sophisticated and easy to use and can be configured to support access by users with different levels of expertise and interest.

- *Adaptability refers to the local context and conditions and the capacity of the tools to be utilized.* These tools include existing databases and 3D models as well as new 3D models, data, and performance indicators. The tools should also be capable of accommodating and supporting a range of possible situations, issues, contexts, and scales (e.g., from a block to a neighborhood and region).

- *Affordability of software and hardware is becoming less of a problem.* In the period between 1990 and 2007 most activities that used to be done on a heavy nonportable Unix and subsequently PC workstations have come to be accomplished on a laptop with a decent graphics card and a portable projector. The larger issues are the data required, training and maintenance, and the requisite time and labor. If the labor costs are high, it begs the question of whether there are better uses of limited resources.

Qualitative Indicators

Performance Report Card

Goal: **Pedestrian Friendly**

- Walkable

- **Nice Walk**
  - Shady
  - Street Wall
  - Transparency

Value-Based Assumptions

Nice Walk

- Walking in the shade is twice as important to Houstonians as walking near a streetwall

- If there is no streetwall, transparency does not matter

Qualitative Indicators can be:

Absolute: (response based)	A nice walk or not a nice walk (yes/no)
Interval: (response based)	• Nice walk • Average walk • Unpleasant walk
Disaggregated: (quantified from environmental indicators)	Nice walk = Shade + Streetwall + Transparency

Figure 4.1 – A component of Houston's Near Northside Economic Revitalization Plan was the formulation of Urban Design Guidelines and a Performance Report Card that would have quantitative as well as qualitative indicators. The goal of "pedestrian friendliness" of the neighborhood could be measured by quantitative indicators, such as "walkable," and qualitative indicators, such as "nice walk." "Walkable" is easily quantified by the distance to the nearest transit stop, presence of sidewalks, etc. But "nice walk," which is qualitative, is more difficult to measure objectively. Photomontages such as those on the left (Images courtesy of Urban Advantage) and 3D simulations are useful in illustrating what is meant by a nice walk, but many qualities that the illustration captures can be disaggregated into more specific, measurable components that are place-specific and value-based, such as "shade," "streetwall," and "transparency." (Indicators courtesy of Environmental Simulation Center, 2001)

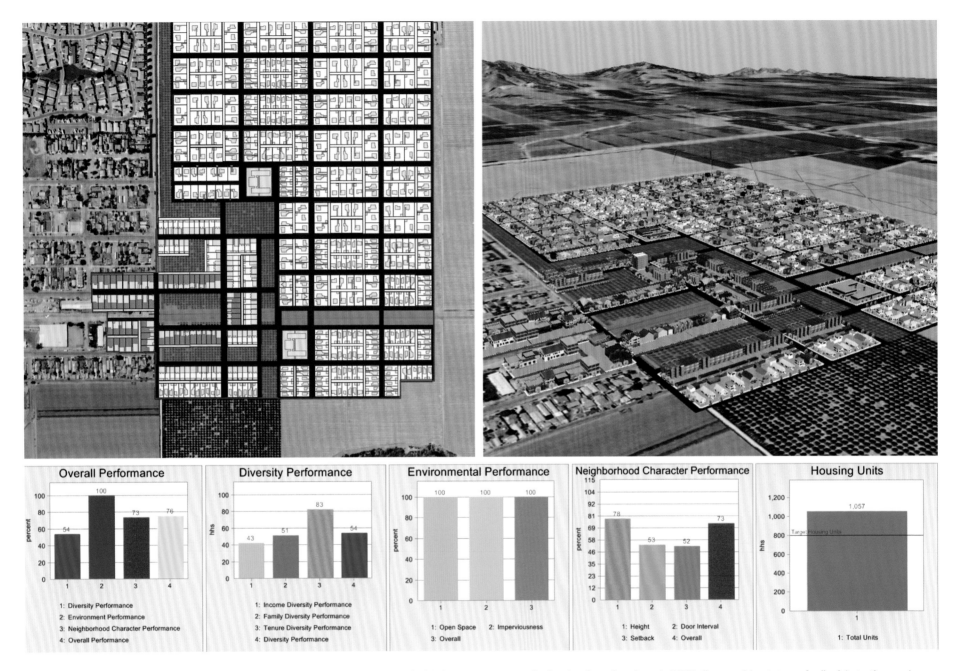

Figure 4.2 – During a Lincoln Institute workshop in California, each group of participants was asked to first formulate then rank performance indicators and second to use those indicators to evaluate the performance of their plans to accommodate anticipated new growth in the Central Valley region. The figure illustrates the CommunityViz™ interface where Scenario 360™ allows participants to see feedback instantly on various performance indicators while visualizing their designs in SiteBuilder 3D™. (Environmental Simulation Center, 2006)

- *Data requirements may vary from software to software.* What is most important is the capacity of the tools to provide useable and meaningful results while minimizing the investment in data. This is particularly important for communities that are just beginning to create their spatial databases, and supports collecting data on "need to know" and "how close is good enough?" bases. This approach incrementally establishes the value of data and information. Data-heavy tools, while sophisticated, may prove to be too costly and difficult both to use and to update on a regular basis.

- *Tool stability, updating, and maintenance can be problematic.* Tools are changing constantly, so it is critical to think ahead and anticipate whether the data and libraries of information created under one tool can easily be transferred and used in another tool. Tool stability is another issue. Most software is never fully debugged, since the manufacturers do not always take responsibility for a tool's instability. The user, in effect, becomes the product tester, identifying bugs and flaws for the software's designers. It is a good policy to avoid initial releases in preference for software that has a large user base. The size of the user pool will tend to determine the continuing updates of the software and its maintenance.

APPLYING THE TOOLS TO THE TASKS

The selection of tools referred to in this section is not exhaustive. The tools cited here are some of those more commonly used for planning, urban design, and visioning. They range from the very straightforward to the extremely complex and sophisticated.

The tasks described below are characteristic of visioning, planning, and design workshops, as well as project review, ongoing planning decision making, implementation, and public information.

Visualizing Existing Conditions

GIS   GIS is arguably the most important tool in the toolbox because it is both the database of existing conditions and the platform on which most PDDSS tools are built (e.g., Community Viz™, INDEX, and PLACE³S). GIS supports a range of applications including, but not limited to:

- capturing a moment in time and changes over time as the database is periodically updated;

- sequential, criteria-based analyses (queries) such as those performed on the Lower Manhattan database (box 4.1);

- 2D and 3D thematic mapping that connects data to a place and a specific visualization project; and

- incorporating information and analyses about both existing and future conditions into reports.

Typically, GIS databases are static and represent a moment in time. It is not unusual for a database to have wildly disparate spatial data, much of it collected over different time periods with varying degrees of accuracy. Understanding the limits of GIS and other databases is critical in interpreting information. The quality of decisions is only as good as the information upon which they are based; however, not all information needs to be of the same quality and freshness.

For communities with a nascent GIS, start-up can appear to be a daunting task, although few PDDSS tools require significant GIS data in order to begin the process. For example, the United States Geological Survey (USGS) provides topographic information for all locations in the United States, albeit with 10-foot contours at best. Similarly, Google Earth™ and other online services provide orthographic aerial and oblique photographs (those that show the façades of the buildings) as well as the ability to extrude 3D models from the photographs.

Working with a small data set may limit the sophistication of what can be done. Nonetheless, it will provide the community with useful information and the ability to make thematic maps that show relationships between information (e.g., slopes, natural drainage systems, and soils) and visualize them in 3D. Once the GIS has proven its worth, the incentive is provided to create other data layers related to problems requiring more data. In addition to planning departments, many public agencies usually find value in the GIS, and thus the cost of creating and sustaining it can be shared by many public agencies that contribute to, share, and update the information.

Box 4.1 Modeling Lower Manhattan

In the early 1990s, with more than 25 million out of approximately 125 million square feet of its office space vacant, Lower Manhattan was in distress and at a crossroads. It was uncertain whether the area should promote the adaptive reuse of whole buildings or merely portions of buildings.

To facilitate an understanding of the potential adaptive reuse of office buildings a Unix-based, floor-by-floor 3D CAD model of Lower Manhattan was created using fire underwriters' maps, architectural drawings, and photographs. The 3D model was linked to an Oracle database that had about twenty fields of data assembled from a variety of sources, including floor-by-floor vacancy, building systems (e.g., number of independent elevator banks and zoning information). Some of the fields, such as floor sizes, adjacencies (e.g., public parks and plazas), building heights, and overbuilt and underbuilt characteristics, were directly filled in by querying the 3D model zoning (figure 4.3).

This proto-3D GIS was probably the first of its kind with floor-by-floor accuracy and detail. The illustrations in figure 4.4 represent a sample of how the 3D GIS was used, in this instance, to determine the potential adaptive reuse to residential use of office buildings in Lower Manhattan. The query was done in a sequence, first applying reasonable criteria regarding floor sizes and heights above the area's canyon-like streets. This query yielded all of the floors in Lower Manhattan that met the criteria. Each building's qualifying floors were summarized and totaled by building, subdistrict, zoning district, and Lower Manhattan. The second step was to determine the path of least resistance to the conversion of commercial office building floors to residential use, based on whether the floors identified were more than 50 percent

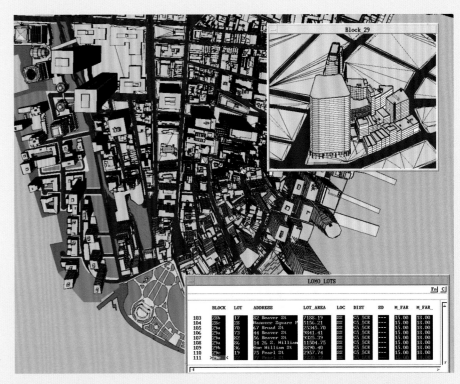

Figure 4.3 – Data was linked to 3D models of Lower Manhattan (Environmental Simulation Center, 1993)

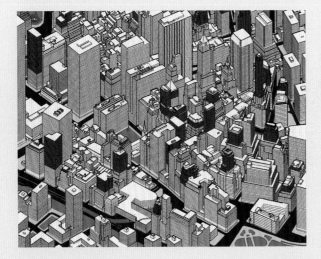

Figure 4.4 – Planning for adaptive reuse in Lower Manhattan using 3D GIS. The left image shows in red all floors above 150 feet that met the criteria for residential reuse; the center image shows in blue only those floors in buildings built prior to 1945; and the right image shows in magenta all floors in pre-1945 buildings that were more than 50 percent vacant. (Environmental Simulation Center, 1993)

Visioning and Visualization

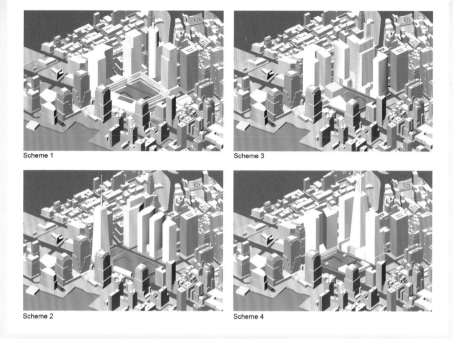

Scheme 1   Scheme 3

Scheme 2   Scheme 4

Figure 4.5 – A 3D model of Lower Manhattan was used as the base model for the four original schemes and all subsequent schemes for the World Trade Center site. (Environmental Simulation Center with Beyer Blinder Belle Architects, 2002)

vacant. The third query in this sequence was policy related, identifying which floors were in buildings built prior to 1945, leaving the post-1945 buildings as a resource for future commercial occupancy.

The usefulness of the third dimension exists in its ability to help the user see areawide patterns of potential adaptive reuse, visualize a vertical mix of uses in former single-use buildings, quantify the potential for adaptive reuse, and spatially reference the data tables. The combination of the 3D representation and tabular information was extremely helpful in understanding spatially where a critical mass of conversions might occur.

The 3D CAD model and Oracle database created for the Lower Manhattan project were exported to GIS when advancements in GIS led to 3D GIS, and it has continued to be used in the planning of post-9/11 Lower Manhattan, including Ground Zero (figure 4.5). It was used in the Regional Plan Association's community workshop on the future of Lower Manhattan, and more recently the Greenwich Street South Urban Design Plan (a collaboration of H³, ESC, Olin Partnership, and Weisz + Yoes; figure 4.6).

The model has been used to create figure-ground maps to visualize the distance and openness between buildings at selected elevations and to create shadow analyses to identify and conserve areas that are sunny in existing and proposed open spaces (figure 4.7). It has also been used for a soft-site analysis to identify possible sites or assemblages for new building development alternatives for Greenwich Street South, by querying the 3D GIS database for buildings that were underbuilt by descending percentages and then displayed in three dimensions.

Figure 4.6 – While developing the Greenwich Street South Urban Design Plan, the design team used the 3D model of existing conditions to determine areas in the district that had sustained solar access, thereby informing the location and heights of buildings. This analysis was performed iteratively as the planning progressed. (Environmental Simulation Center, 2004)

Figure 4.7 – The 3D CAD massing models of Lower Manhattan were converted to a real-time 3D simulation with textures applied to the façades of the buildings. The model was used interactively during the development of the Greenwich Street South Urban Design Plan to visualize design alternatives for proposed new structures and a large public park. (Environmental Simulation Center, 2004)

Although the information in GIS is static, changes over time can be recorded and analyzed. GIS can also be used to collect and spatially locate qualitative as well as traditional quantitative information. In the case of a Hope VI project to improve conditions in a public housing project in New York City, the ESC used GIS in conjunction with its version of the "Good Places/Bad Places" exercise to record tenant, police, and social service providers' perceptions of the project

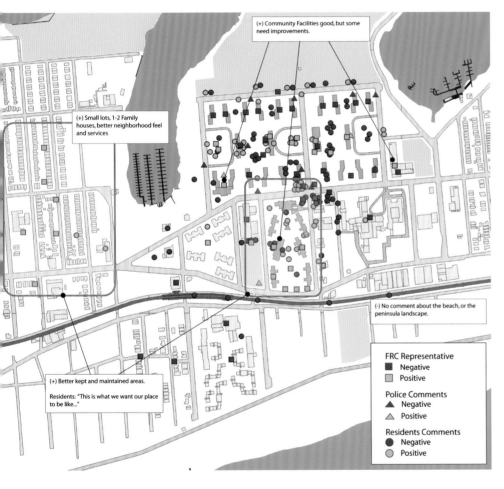

Figure 4.8 – Perceptions of their neighborhood from residents, police officers, and social service providers were recorded using GIS in the HOPE VI Good Places/Bad Places exercise (for the Averne and Edgemere Houses in Queens, New York). The use of GIS enabled the design team to clearly identify conflicting and concurring perceptions, suggest initial interventions, and assess the effectiveness of those interventions based on changing stakeholder perceptions. (Environmental Simulation Center, 2001)

and its neighborhood (figure 4.8). Placing green and red dots (with the participants' names keyed to the dots) on an aerial photograph of the area allowed for a better understanding of where there was consensus and where there were conflicting perceptions (often between young and old tenants, and residents and police). Identified conflicts were then discussed among the stakeholders and often resolved. In the long term, these maps will be used to track the changes in perception resulting from design interventions by repeating the "Good Places/ Bad Places" exercise periodically and updating the maps. These maps are also intended to be used to hold management and their architects accountable for their actions and to inform future interventions.

3D GIS Applications Three-dimensional displays of information may be static images of a 3D model and database, or dynamic visualizations where the user can literally and freely move through the virtual environment in real time. Because we experience the world in three dimensions in time and motion, adding the third dimension can be extremely helpful in assisting stakeholders in better understanding that which they are viewing. This may be done by connecting a 3D CAD model to a GIS or other database, or more recently to GIS-based 3D visualization software and applications. In fact, seeing things in two dimensions may be misleading until you see it in three dimensions. Seeing is not always believing! Visualizing neighborhood information can also help tie abstract information, such as census data and maps, directly to place (figure 4.9).

Asset maps are thematic 3D maps that can be used to communicate neighborhood change and activity, tying together often disparate thematic information (figure 4.10). Because the 3D models are being used to display information, the 3D models of buildings are represented as massing models.

A 3D GIS can be extremely helpful in visualizing information and queries that otherwise would be difficult to understand in maps and tabular and graphic outputs. For example, mixed-use districts can be understood more easily in the third dimension; in a given district the buildings may house a variety of uses (e.g., residential, retail, office), which are difficult to display effectively on two-dimensional maps.

When trying to convey perceptual information, such as what it would be like to walk down a street, massing models may be appropriate when used analytically, but may be too abstract at the experiential level of a pedestrian (box 4.2). They

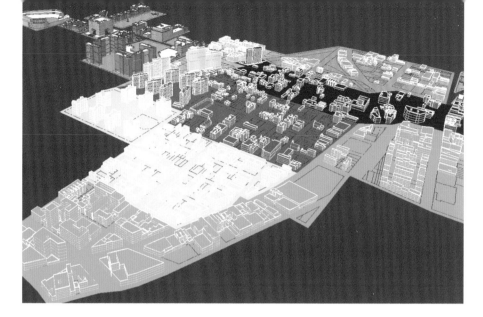

Figure 4.9 – Census tracts laid over a 3D model of the Melrose Commons area of the South Bronx in New York City. (Environmental Simulation Center, 1996)

Figure 4.10 – Community asset map of Melrose Commons, South Bronx, New York City. (Environmental Simulation Center, 1996)

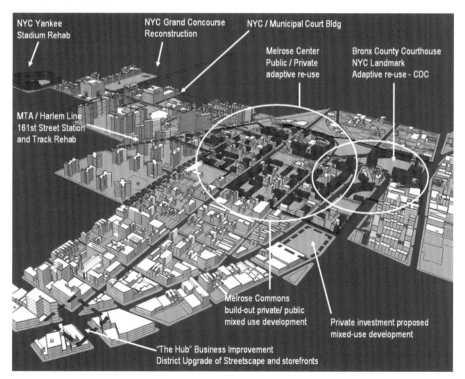

have little of the detail and texture that one typically finds on buildings when walking through a neighborhood. Realism can be achieved through more detailed 3D models or through the use of photographs that are "pasted" onto the massing model. While this type of 3D model can be used statically, its real value is in the virtual 3D reality environment, where the participants can freely navigate in the world of the model.

How the future is modeled is critical to keeping the discussion focused on the choices. For example, in situations where the issues concern planning and urban design rather than the specific design of a building, then site planning, building massing, and streetscape design are the issues that need to be framed for public discussion. The use of existing buildings in a neighborhood or district that is familiar to the participants and not distracting allows the discussion to focus on urban design and site planning alternatives (rather than the architectural design of the buildings)—in an "apples-to-apples" comparison that can utilize the same 3D models. The architectural quality of the buildings used in the 3D model is not the issue, at least at this point in the process (figure 4.11).

Designing and Visualizing Alternatives

So far we have discussed only 3D models of existing conditions. The application of visualization tools goes well beyond that, making the design of a region, town, neighborhood, or public place—previously the domain of urban designers and planners—accessible to everyone.

The visioning process is always rooted in the world of everyday experience. The places inhabited and used by people have a direct relationship to collective and individual values and sense of identity. The design of place is critical to the concept of visioning, which advocates the view that design matters by translating policy choices into design choices. Further, visioning assumes that there are many "right" answers to a problem, or responses to a particular policy. Through design one may question the policy itself, or the way the issue has been framed, as the implications of the policy are "played out on the ground."

Christopher Alexander explains this process in *Notes on the Synthesis of Form* (1966) in which he presents teacups that perform their function but emphasize different priorities, resulting in the enormous range of teacups that have been designed over many centuries. While there is no perfect teacup, there are many wonderful teacups.

Figure 4.11 – 3D visualizations show two different site plans for a gas station/convenience store in the Houston Near Northside Economic Revitalization Plan. The figure above shows the typical arrangement, with the pump area at the corner and the convenience store in back. The figure below shows an alternative plan, where the convenience store is moved to the corner, creating more pedestrian-friendly conditions. By using the same typical buildings in both versions, the discussion is focused on site planning rather than architecture. (Environmental Simulation Center, 2001)

The design process is a combination of problem solving and the application of intuition. Designs are characteristically based on a program that is both quantitative (e.g., the amount of building floor area to be accommodated) and qualitative (e.g., creating a pleasant, engaging, and safe pedestrian environment). Typically alternatives are developed that address both the quantitative and qualitative program requirements, but in different ways and and with varying emphases. The

Box 4.2 A 3D Massing Model of the Cathedral Church of St. John the Divine

Three-dimensional models can be used analytically to explain a pedestrian's visual experience dynamically. In the example of the Cathedral Church of St. John the Divine in Manhattan, a 3D massing model was constructed of the cathedral and the surrounding blocks. A massing model built from drawings of the cathedral was chosen as having the appropriate level of information to help the public and the city's Landmark Preservation Commission understand how the cathedral and its close are perceived by a pedestrian (figure 4.12).

Dubbed "seeing and perceiving," the exercise consisted of a digital pedestrian, with the equivalent of a miner's hat with a large flashlight, who walked the perimeter of the cathedral with her light focused on the cathedral. As she moved down the street in real time, the areas of the cathedral shown in white were those that the pedestrian saw at a given moment during the walk. The visualization analysis showed that the spacing of the existing buildings along the close's perimeter framed, and thereby heightened, the viewer's experience of the key aspects of the cathedral (crossing, towers, apse, nave), if only for fleeting moments. This flow of information, during which the cathedral is seen intermittently, led to the viewer's composite perception of the cathedral, notwithstanding how little she actually saw physiologically. In this example, such dynamic analytical techniques helped the public and the Landmark Preservation Commission appreciate how the spatial organization of existing buildings on the close enhanced the viewers' experience of the cathedral.

A number of digital techniques were explored. The viewshed analysis software in GIS was used first, but was not particularly useful because it was based on line of sight. The 3D display only showed static views from a particular location to a selected object point and only visualized what could be seen and not what could not be seen, rendering the visualization process is iterative, where the designers in a series of steps analyze, evaluate, and refine the "fit" between each of the design alternatives and the program during which the designer learns what works and what does not.

An example of the integration of problem solving and intuition in the creative process is Frank Lloyd Wright's house Fallingwater in rural Pennsylvania, which perches above a waterfall. The house is improbable in two respects. First, if site

contextless, since you could not see the whole cathedral. Animating line of sight proved to be daunting and was rejected since the GIS software was not developed to be animated. Instead, the CAD model of the cathedral was transported to 3D Studio, a sophisticated animation package that provided the ESC with the tools for the analysis (e.g., movement, levels of transparency and opaqueness, and lighting).

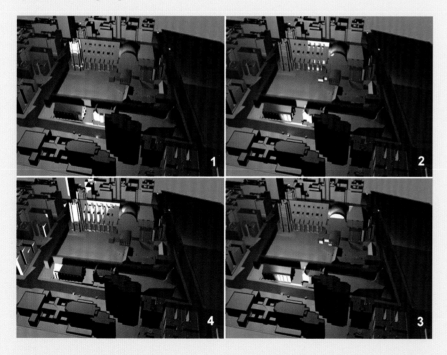

Figure 4.12 – "Seeing and Perceiving": Time-lapse screen captures (clockwise, from top left) highlight the portions of the cathedral as they would be seen by a pedestrian walking around the cathedral. (Environmental Simulation Center, 2004)

selection were by deduction, a site immediately atop a waterfall probably would not have made it through a deductive site-suitability analysis. Second, cantilevering the house over the waterfall so that you don't see it but hear it is equally improbable. Regardless of how seemingly counterintuitive the siting of the house is, both the site and the house are, when experienced, surprising, logically executed, and wonderful. This is an example of "the good you couldn't think of."

Unlike traditional urban, architectural, and landscape design, design as used in the visioning process is a form of inquiry, whether it be at the large scale, such as a region, county, or city (responding to the question, where do we grow?), or at the experiential scale of a district, corridor, or neighborhood (investigating how do we grow?).

Design as inquiry is based on the educational concept of learning by doing. It may involve the placing of a development chip on a map in the Where Do We Grow? exercise, or creating a streetscape through the choice and placement of 3D buildings in the How Do We Grow? exercise, or assembling alternative development scenarios from prototypical development patterns (see Baltimore case study in chapter 6). The learning is experienced through the objective evaluation of one's design decisions or choices by seeing how well that choice performed against one's own indicators.

Design as inquiry is also facilitated by the use of information technology. It provides the means by which laypeople can design places and visually experience the results of their efforts dynamically, enabling them to walk through their design at eye level in a virtual reality 3D environment. By definition, design in this context is about making informed choices and solving problems. This assessment is critical to both the design and the learning process because it provides feedback as one designs in either two or three dimensions. In this modality, design is an iterative process where the feedback loops made possible by the use of information technology support multiple iterations in which both the design and the performance indicators used to evaluate the design can be modified on the fly (box 4.3).

The tools described in this section focus on design as an exercise in exploring what-if scenarios. Design reasoning is supported by both 2D and 3D representation, as well as tabular information in databases such as GIS. The discussion begins with basic tools such as visual preference surveys and digital photomontages and proceeds to the application of sophisticated PDDSS tools such as CommunityViz™ and INDEX.

Visual Preferences Surveys These surveys utilize photographs of situations in a comparative analysis to elicit stakeholder responses. Typically the survey is done with matching sets of photographs—one of existing conditions and one of how the conditions might be addressed through design. The alternatives are sometimes from other communities, but can and should be local when local examples are available.

Care must be exercised when using comparative photographs, because photographs are rich visual environments with information ranging from the superfluous to the essential. Moreover, the photographs themselves can be biased: they may be interestingly or uninterestingly framed by the camera, show differences of color and light, communicate time and type of day (cloudy, sunny, etc.), and they may or may not show human activity. All of these variables make it difficult to understand to which factors the stakeholders are responding.

Box 4.3 **The Medium Is the Message**

All media are loaded in the McLuhan sense that "the medium is the message" (McLuhan 1967). Notwithstanding their inherent limitations, the tools used should be able to promote the identification of design options. This may be as simple as static photomontages that illustrate what the design options are or tools that are intuitive and interactive, that encourage the user to try things, preferably by building an environment in two and three dimensions.

When coupled with impact analysis and performance evaluation on the fly, they inform the user as a vision develops. In this instance, design options emerge from an iterative learning process. The visual simulation of design choices, whether in static 2D/3D or dynamic virtual reality 3D, is critical because the physical design of a place is policy and may be realized and experienced in the real world. It is also an excellent way to test policies by comparing the design of place with the policy statements and the performance indicators that articulate the policies and principles in quantitative and qualitative terms.

This is what is meant by working in a nonlinear, nonhierarchical fashion. Rather than use images (whether static or dynamic) to illustrate policies by going from the abstraction of policies in descending order to what it would look like, this approach starts with the specifics of a place as implicit policy or policy-realized, and works at multiple scales simultaneously, integrating actions at all scales.

Visual preferences surveys can be valuable for getting a sense of stakeholder values and identity. The downside is that those values and identities with which stakeholders identify may often be manipulated by the marketplace, which also uses imagery to influence people's attitudes and values.

Digital Photomontages Photomontages are always place specific, illustrate what-ifs in an experiential environment, frame choices, and can serve as armatures for informed discussions among stakeholders on planning, urban design, and public policy issues. Typically, photomontages show existing conditions and alternatives for the future either at the eye level of a pedestrian, as aerial views, or both (figure 4.13).

There are two types of digital photomontages, nonverifiable and verifiable. In a nonverifiable photomontage the illustrator, using photograph manipulation software, has inserted into a photograph of existing conditions images of buildings or streetscape elements as placeholders for a design/planning/policy intervention. These photographs are corrected for size, scale, and perspective, so that the resulting image feels right to a viewer. Creating convincing digital photomontages is an art, requiring a well-trained eye.

Digital photomontages are extremely helpful in giving concrete form to concepts, which is often difficult for laypeople and decision makers to do if they lack the skills to translate policies, ideas, and words into real-world environments at an urban scale. Eye-level digital photomontages are particularly effective because they can help citizens internalize what is represented and then go to the location in the photograph or photomontage and imagine the future. This last step is important because, unlike a photograph that is static, the real world is dynamic, changing all the time, and certainly is a richer environment than a photograph or digital photomontage can simulate.

Although digital montages of this type are relatively inexpensive to create, they are limited in that they are purely visual and experiential. Montages can neither be verified (e.g., regarding dimensions) nor queried for nonvisual information (e.g., density, floor area by use, number of dwelling units). Verifiable photomontages are dimensionally accurate, and because they are constructed using CAD-based 3D modeling they may also include attribute data that can be queried (e.g., information attached to the 3D models in the scene such as use and floor areas).

Verifiability becomes important when stakeholders agree that the images are what they like, and then need to understand how to implement them and to comprehend the implications of operating in an imperfect world. This level of verifiability often requires that a queryable database that includes attribute data be attached to the alternatives illustrated in the digital photomontage.

A verifiable digital photomontage is constructed of existing and proposed buildings or structures in a 3D CAD massing model that is dimensionally and spatially accurate. Simulating the camera lens in the CAD software and replicating the actual viewpoint from which the photograph was taken creates a perspective view from that location. (Fifty- to fifty-five-millimeter lenses show actual distances and relative displacement as most people would see them and are the accepted standard for converting from lens to perspective.) The perspective view is then adjusted to be isomorphic or coincident with the key buildings, structures, or landscape elements in the photograph, making the proposed structures and buildings dimensionally verifiable.

If the image is to be queryable, then a database needs to be linked to the CAD model so it can be queried. For example, if an illustration were to be made verifiable, it would require another level of design and decision, as the façades in the photomontage are just that, façades like those on a movie set, with nothing behind them and, as in the movies, utterly convincing. To move from a façade to a series of buildings, parks, and other elements requires another level of design decision making that is able to support interactive design in an information-rich environment.

Figure 4.13 – A digital photomontage showing before and after conditions of proposed transit-oriented development in San Jose, California. (Images courtesy of Urban Advantage)

2D and 3D Design and Visualization Tools   3D design and visualization tools provide the means to explore the implications of design ideas and concepts in a virtual world and to evaluate their performance against values held by the community. This section examines the leading 2D and 3D PDDSS tools (CommunityViz™, INDEX, and Paint the Region) that support the public involvement process (box 4.4).

Box 4.4 The Application of 3D Tools at Princeton Junction

The value of 3D visual simulation should not be underestimated. There is very often a mismatch between what people say and the image they have in their mind's eye. An early ESC project was to visualize the words and numbers in a master plan for a stakeholder workshop. The first thing workshop participants wanted to do after seeing the plan visually simulated was to modify it and develop other alternatives—a natural response. To accommodate this anticipated need, a LEGO™-like generic 3D kit of parts was created that could be used both to visualize quickly the master plan, and could be used to modify the visualization on the fly (figure 4.14). The kit of parts was given characteristics that could help verify that the representation was consistent with the master plan, and quantitative goals and objectives, and that in subsequent iterations the new alternatives could be quantified for the workshop participants. Attributing the 3D kit of parts kept participants accountable for their choices.

The response to the visual simulation of the master plan revealed that the participants were not happy with the initial visualization. There was a mismatch between what the participants wanted and what the master plan described in words and numbers. Using the 3D kit of parts in real time, the participants modified the original plan, altering earlier rules to reflect their values. The ability to translate the master plan quickly into three dimensions and then modify the 3D model could only have been efficiently and cost-effectively accomplished with a flexible toolkit of building and landscape components. This prototype, done in CAD with attribute data and visual simulation software, was proof of concept that such a tool was possible and that it was much needed to close the gap between what the stakeholders said and what they really wanted.

Designing in three dimensions in real time has been made possible through application of PDDSS tools such as CommunityViz™, built on ESRI's ArcView, a GIS platform. It has a real-time virtual reality component, a scenario constructor, and impact analysis tools. Using a similar kit of parts of 3D buildings, public open spaces, and block lot and road types with attributes (e.g., use, density, family type, vehicle speeds), a participant can quickly design a prototypical place and get instantaneous feedback as to how well they are meeting the agreed-upon program and their own performance indicators. The linking of the kit of parts to data, program, and performance indicators makes design both accountable and discussable in a public format. The ability literally to create what-ifs in three dimensions is both a learning and decision-making process, brought about by the stakeholders' understanding of the implications of design choices (figure 4.15).

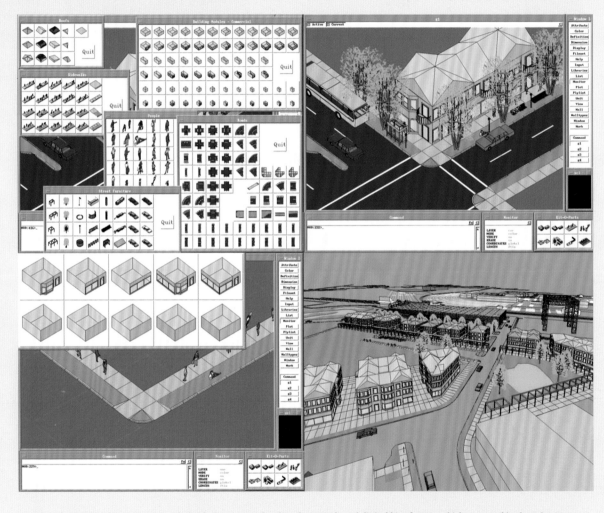

Figure 4.14 – In 1994 the Environmental Simulation Center developed a UNIX-based digital kit of parts, which was used in the Princeton Junction, New Jersey, transit-oriented development workshop to create alternatives by assembling roads, blocks, and buildings in real time.

Smart Building Kit of Parts

MU2

6 Story Apts. with Penthouse
and Ground Floor Retail

55 Families
Owner: 0
Rental: 15 – 1 BR, 38 – 2 BR, 2 – 3 BR
Building Floor Area= 35,150 SF
Typical Length 90–100 ft.   Typical Depth 60–65 ft.
Parking: Covered

MU1

6 Story Apts. with Elevator at 2 Flats per floor
and Ground Floor Retail

10 Families
Owner: 10 – 2 BR
Rental: 0
Building Floor Area= 12,900 SF
Typical Length 45–50 ft.   Typical Depth 45–55 ft.
Parking: Covered

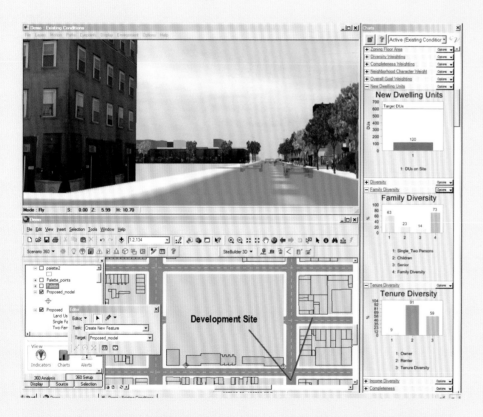

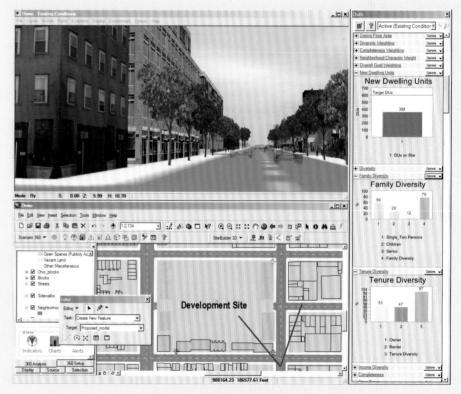

Figure 4.15 – Planning and designing in real time. Examples of smart building kit parts and some of their attributes that have been used in community planning and design workshops are shown above. The combination of smart buildings and stakeholder-derived indicators and benchmarks provides the context in which workshop participants can generate "what-if?" scenarios quickly by selecting and placing the building models in the context and evaluate their performance on the fly (left: site before building placement; right: site after placing buildings). (Environmental Simulation Center, 2004)

attribute data and provide feedback loops that the stakeholders can use to analyze and frame choices. If people play these games for fun, we asked ourselves, couldn't PDDSS tools capture the public's interest in cities and design of place by creating a virtual environment in which it would be fun and engaging to plan and design a real-world community?

CommunityViz™ is a multifunctional tool based on a GIS platform where visual simulations in 3D can be tied to GIS data, new policies can be proposed, and alternate scenarios modeled in both 2D and 3D. Conversely, alternative scenarios can be designed directly in the 2D/3D environment and the implicit policies extracted. The impacts of the alternatives can be quickly quantified by subjecting each alternative to evaluation by performance indicators based on principles formulated by stakeholders. Most important, everything can be viewed and modified on the fly in an interactive process in which the stakeholders learn by doing (figure 4.17).

CommunityViz™ is a suite of integrated software tools that supports spatial decision making and analysis of land use scenarios. It enables a community to view, project, analyze, and understand potential changes to its town. CommunityViz™ is comprised of two components: Scenario 360™ and SiteBuilder 3D™. They interact with each other to reflect any changes made to either one.

Scenario 360™ is an interactive tool for performing impact analysis of alternative development scenarios. It uses the basic elements of performance indicators, scenarios, attributes, variables, constants, and analysis. It updates attributes, monitors constraints, and tracks performance indicators as the user changes land use parameters or underlying assumptions. It also allows users without a technical background to build and evaluate a multitude of both predefined and customized scenarios using a 3D kit of building blocks.

Figure 4.16 – Inspiration for CommunityViz™ came from two computer games: SimCity™ and LEGO Creator™.

SiteBuilder 3D™ is an interactive, real-time 3D environment. It provides a generic set of attributed building models or kit of building blocks (e.g., number of dwelling units, uses per floor, zoning, total floor area) to create and dynamically update a 3D representation of the stakeholders' community and/or alternative development scenarios. In addition, new attributed building blocks can be created in software such as Sketchup™.

INDEX and Paint the Region are primarily 2D design tools that can be linked to 3D models to create real-time environments. Like other PDDSS tools, INDEX is built on a GIS platform. By also employing Paint the Region software and a

The support of the design process and inquiry through design in an engaging, nonlinear, nonhierarchical PDDSS tool has been the goal of the ESC and other designers. The inspiration for the development of CommunityViz™ draws on SimCity™, one of the most popular computer games in the world today, and on LEGO™ (LEGO Creator™ is a digital version of LEGO™), one of the most popular building toys (figure 4.16). Both games reflect continuing interest in cities and how cities happen. SimCity™, a public policy game, supports the planning process. LEGO Creator™, a design game, enables the intuitive design of buildings and places. Both tools are "smart," in that they have embedded digital drawing tablet, stakeholders can literally draw a plan for an entire community using the "dial-in palette" by importing neighborhood layouts, populating them with building types, coloring in land uses, and using other functions (figure 4.18). The building types are proxies for the densities and urban design characteristics of the portion of the transect being designed. The building types are represented in photographs and supported by an array of information about each building type—floor area, occupancy, employment, number of units, valuation, etc.—that provides data for the design alternatives, which are then used to evaluate the performance of a design alternative in real time similar to CommunityViz™ (figure 4.19).

While the preferred display in a workshop setting of Paint the Region is a digital drawing tablet around which stakeholders can gather, a display can also be used on a computer screen. Either type of display requires a knowledgeable operator to execute the stakeholder choices, thus diminishing the spontaneity made possible by drawing directly on the digital tablet. In this regard, it is similar to CommunityViz™, which also requires an experienced operator. The primary advantage of the tablet is that it supports face-to-face design decision making unlike the monitor, which requires the stakeholders to gather around the screen.

Notwithstanding the visualization medium (tablet or monitor), the use of proxies has limitations. The proxies require that the user imagine walking

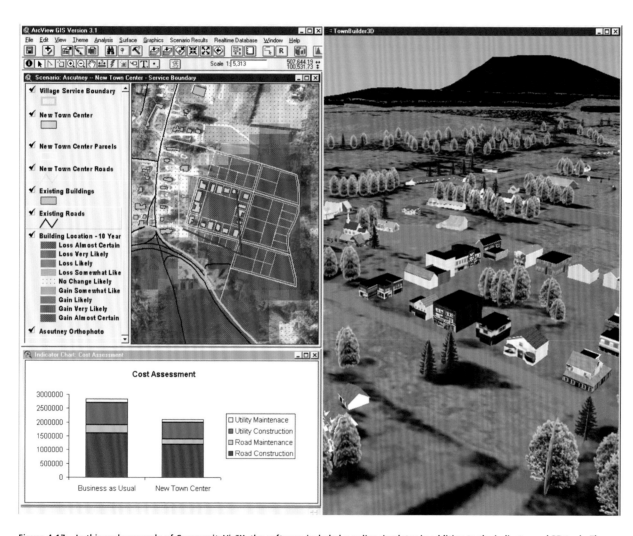

Figure 4.17 – In this early example of CommunityViz™, the software included a policy simulator in addition to the indicator and 3D tools. The policy being simulated is for the creation of a new town center with infrastructure. The blue areas on the map indicate the degree to which individuals in the simulation choose to live and work in the town center. (Environmental Simulation Center, 1999)

Figure 4.18 – The INDEX PlanBuilder interface has a palette of "paintable" land uses and shows a tabulation of growth painted. (Courtesy of Criterion Planners, Inc.)

through the alternative and internalize the imagery, visualizing in her mind's eye what the entire district or community would look and feel like where the ensemble is greater than the sum of individual building choices. This is not an easy task for either laypeople or professionals who lack design experience.

3D Modeling   Up to this point we have discussed location-specific design interventions. There are situations in which the issues combine both policy and design and where design is used to test policies. In this type of situation it is often desirable not to simulate an actual place visually, but to create a representative place that stakeholders recognize but cannot specifically locate. This is intentional, as the issue concerns not a specific piece of property but an entire class of properties (e.g., a neighborhood or district) and the impact changes in policy would have on the existing character of the place.

To create a representative series of blocks in a neighborhood one needs to understand the visual organization of the block. This will include block, street, sidewalk, and lot size and dimensions, as well as the building types and landscape elements that would accrue to the different lot sizes. By sampling the GIS, a series of blocks representative of lot sizes, frontages, and building footprints and photorealistic 3D buildings can be created in a 3D model that has the look and feel of the neighborhood, except that the figurative deck of cards has been shuffled.

For example, the Steamboat Springs, Colorado, community had the choice of either increasing the allowable zoning density of the neighborhood to accommodate infill development and additions to existing buildings, or expanding the town's boundaries to accommodate the anticipated growth. The 3D real-time model of the representative blocks was used to visualize the impact that an increase in density would have on the character of the neighborhood, and to explain the relationship among the zoning ordinances' floor area ratio (FAR), height, and coverage restrictions (figure 4.20). FAR is a multiplier of the lot area that determines the amount of floor area a building may have.

A range of FARs was visualized in the real-time 3D model, allowing the planning commissioners and stakeholders to move freely through the model, turning alternative FARs and their physical

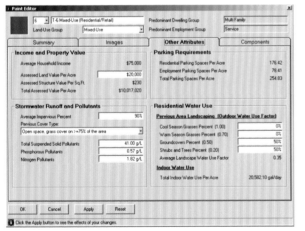
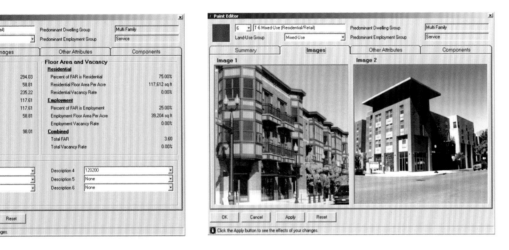
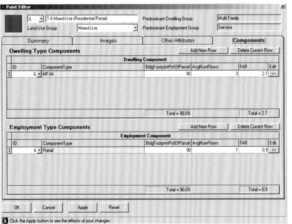

Figure 4.19 – One of the development types selected from the INDEX PlanBuilder palette shows (clockwise from upper left) summary demographic information, examples of what this type of development might look like, mixed-use components, and other attributes such as income and property value, storm-water runoff, parking requirments, etc. (Images courtesy of Criterion Planners, Inc.)

  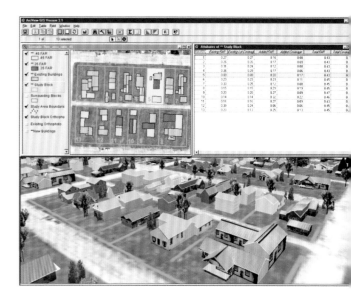

Figure 4.20 – These images illustrate three different FARs (with the maximum lot coverage held constant at 35 percent) on a hypothetical block that is a composite of buildings and lot sizes in the Old Town neighborhood of Steamboat Springs, Colorado. The image on the left visualizes current density at a FAR of .23.

The middle image visualizes what a FAR of .35 would look like. The image on the right visualizes a FAR of .45 and the implications of keeping the maximum lot coverage at 35 percent (the buildings grow vertically rather than horizontally). (Environmental Simulation Center, 1999)

implications on and off. The chart correlated FAR, building height, and coverage to their visual simulation, making the consequences of the words and numbers immediately understandable to both the public and the planning commissioners. In addition to visualizing the community's choices, the real-time walk-through revealed an issue that had escaped attention—snow accumulation. The infill alley houses proposed to absorb future growth and provide affordable housing had been located at the alley lot line. This left little or no space for the up to five feet of snow that might accumulate over the course of the winter, resulting in a required setback for alley houses.

3D Tools: Prepathed and Real-time Animation An animated feature is made up of a 3D environment represented by thousands of complex scenes or sequenced frames of that environment that must be rendered or drawn. It takes a large amount of time to draw every image, sometimes up to 20 minutes per frame depending on the complexity of the scene and the power of the computer doing the rendering. The animator, however, has already decided the sequence of the frames and can prerender them on powerful computers over a period

of days. Since these animations stress realism and special effects, they typically have highly complex scenes with extensive geometric detail, lighting, and shading. Most important, one sees the world through the eyes of the director and editor, where the viewer's eye is the equivalent of the camera's lens. Prepathed animation used in the planning process is most often used at the end of the process to illustrate and sell the plan to the public.

Real-time animation always requires a virtual 3D model in which the user can freely navigate. Unlike prepathed animation, which can also take place in a virtual 3D model, real-time animation is not manipulative; it promotes exploration and learning during the planning and design process. While it can be used in public presentations, it is primarily a learning tool that allows workshop participants to manipulate the objects in the virtual environment (e.g., buildings, landscape and streetscape elements) in real time by moving objects around and/or adding or subtracting objects in the model. This functionality complements and supports scenario construction, where each alternative or scenario can be saved for comparison purposes and, as in the case of CommunityViz™, analyze the impacts.

Figure 4.21 – Rendering a scene in real time requires conservation of system resources. In this example from the Village of Great Neck Plaza, in New York State, the real-time model was only meant to illustrate the main shopping street at eye-level (left), so only the parts of the buildings seen from the street were modeled in geometric detail and with textures (above and below). (Environmental Simulation Center, 2003)

In a real-time animation, the user determines his or her own path while being in the 3D model, in contrast to the predetermined path typical of an animation such as a cartoon. *Real time* refers to a live rendering or drawing time of about 30 frames per second, which is close to simulating our visual experience in real life. Scenes for real time need to be rendered at such speeds because emphasis is placed on enabling an interactive, dynamic experience for the user. The sequence of the scenes being drawn is not determined until the user actually interacts with the environment. Every time the user moves the mouse to change his or her perspective ever so slightly, a new scene must be rendered. In order to simulate a real-time experience, each frame must be drawn as quickly as possible so that movement is smooth and realistic. Such fast rendering times are achieved by minimizing the complexity of the objects and landscape scenes by using photographic imagery.

Typically, the kit of building and landscape blocks is rendered photorealistically, although there are instances where massing models may suffice. For example, a photorealistic 3D building model in the real-time virtual reality model is designed to conserve both modeling and computer processing performance to allow smooth movement through the virtual environment (figure 4.21).

Simply, photographs of existing buildings are then electronically pasted onto the massing model. While the building forms may be simplified, the photographs suggest a wealth of detail, depth, and substance, playing on the way in which people make visual sense of an environment. The difference between seeing (physiological) and perception (psychological) permits us to make assumptions about the physical world around us by generalizing, or filling in the missing blanks. It is a technique effectively derived from film and game special effects, in which movement requires the user to get clues quickly from a flow of information in lieu of the ability to contemplate a static scene such as a painting or photograph.

Evaluating Alternatives

In the previous sections we have discussed creating alternatives or scenarios and visualizing them in 2D and 3D. This section discusses how stakeholders can use the tools to great effect to formulate performance indicators that visually assess alternatives in apples-to-apples comparisons.

Formulating the performance indicators is an integral part of the design process used in visioning. Performance indicators describe our expectations as to how we expect things to work. During the visioning process, the formulation of quantitative and qualitative performance indicators is done by stakeholders prior to the actual designing of alternatives with the 3D kit of building blocks (CommunityViz™) or in 2D (INDEX, Paint the Region). These indicators represent the stakeholders' values and sense of identity and establish the common ground toward which the visioning process strives.

Performance indicators can be both qualitative and quantitative. In a performance system, it is assumed that full compliance is not always achievable, that there are trade offs between performance indicators, therefore partial compliance is acceptable. Further, performance assumes that there are many "right" answers, because performance sets out the problem to be solved when designing alternatives. Typically stakeholders are encouraged to rank the performance indicators because in the real world all things are not necessarily valued equally. The choice is often among incommensurables requiring trade offs (e.g., the conservation of open space versus density, better air quality versus reliance on the automobile), leading to an informed public discussion of values and priorities (figures 4.22 and 4.23).

Most PDDSS tools support the performance evaluation of alternatives. For example, Community Viz™ and INDEX are open systems. This section focuses on PDDSS that are essentially shells that need to be populated by the stakeholders with place-specific variables, performance indicators, benchmarks, and capacities. These PDDSS tools often come with presets or defaults that the stakeholders may or may not choose to adopt, or adapt to their location and issues. It is always preferable that performance indicators reflect the issues, values, and sense of identity of the stakeholders, although it may require a greater investment in project resources.

Performance by indicator is best explained graphically, where one can easily and quickly understand not only a single indicator but also how a series of indicators relate to each other (figure 4.24). When performance measures, capacities, and benchmarks are weighted they represent the relative importance the stakeholders place on them.

When used to evaluate an alternative, weighting reveals which "tail is wagging the dog." For example, assuming x number of housing units are required to meet future demand within a fixed area, there will be a preference between the type, scale, and size of buildings and the amount of open space provided in an alternative. More open space means less area for buildings. The results of the performance evaluation often leads to a reweighting of the indicators to bring them into line with what is perceived by the stakeholders to be preferable. This is a critical step in the process, because indicators and their weighting may also need to be reevaluated along with the alternatives.

When used in conjunction with the real-time 3D visual simulation of alternatives, performance indicators are made palpable to stakeholders (for example, in CommunityViz™). In this environment the stakeholders receive instant feedback as they design alternatives in real time by deploying attributed models from the kit of building blocks into the model. By working this way, the design process becomes iterative, encouraging the fine tuning of the alternatives on the fly. Saving each iteration is important, as it captures the process of design and the decisions being made.

Forecasting is an emerging tool predicated on the concept that the world is dynamic and relationships are always in a state of flux. Unlike traditional impact analysis, which deals with a moment in time, forecasting adds the dimension of time, which generates a flow of information. It always provides a

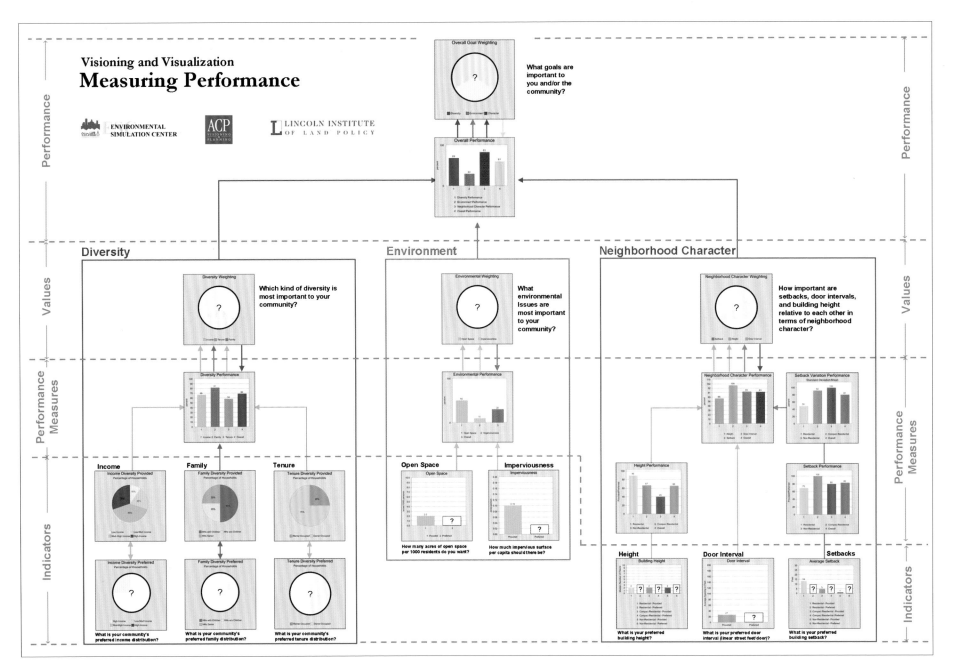

Figure 4.22 – Qualitative and quantitative indicators can be developed to measure performance while the plan is being formulated and over time as it is implemented. The diagram illustrates the categories of diversity, the environment, and neighborhood and how they may be broken into their component parts (e.g., diversity: income, family, tenure), measured for performance in CommunityViz™, and ranked. (California Central Valley Visioning and Visualization Workshop, Lincoln Institute/Environmental Simulation Center, 2006)

Figure 4.23 – A participant at the California Central Valley Workshop presents his group's plan and explains how well it performs against the group's own performance measures. (ACP–Visioning & Planning)

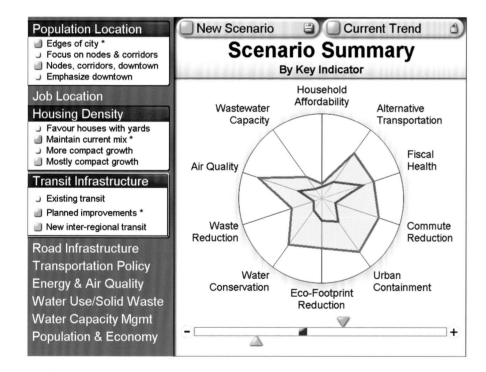

Figure 4.24 – This graph from MetroQuest™ allows users to compare scenarios across each key indicator. The larger the footprint, or closer to the outside of the circle, the better it performs. The slider bar at the bottom summarizes the relative desirability of each scenario. The further to the right, the better it performs. The orange triangle represents the region's current trend, the green triangle represents an alternate possibility, and the blue square represents the base year. (Image courtesy of Envision Sustainability Tools, Inc.)

range of possible outcomes. For example, forecasting can be used to identify, within a range, a tipping point or the equivalent of a change in state, such as when water becomes ice. It may integrate a host of policies and actions, play out the interactions among them, and identify unforeseen consequences that may emerge.

Neighborhood change or gentrification, investment in infrastructure to spur positive change, and the cumulative results of granting variances over time are all examples for which forecasting would be invaluable in a nonepisodic, continuous planning process. Forecasting is particularly valuable when coupled with a vision plan's principles, allowing the community to assess the consistency of its actions with its principles and performance indicators over time.

SUMMARY

The visualization tools presented in this chapter ideally create a level playing field in which all the participants have equal access to information and data. The playing field is leveled even more when the visualization tools are an integral component of a public process that treasures transparency and that blends the intuitive knowledge of participants with the information brought to the table by staff and consultants.

Transparency and the generous availability of understandable information enable the public to make informed and confident decisions and elevate the planning process into a broader exercise of citizenship and stewardship.

5. Implementation

The tools described in chapter 4 enable the development of a comprehensive and coherent plan that fully embodies the ideas and aspirations of the community. The plan must be implemented, however, and the vision of the community has to become reality.

The process of implementation follows the same iterative steps as the development of the plan. Public involvement continues in ways that are both formal—such as developing regulatory tools to enable the plan's implementation—and informal, through the creation of task forces empowered to implement, or monitor the implementation of, discrete elements of the plan.

A plan created with strong public involvement establishes the context for implementation in three important ways. First, it articulates the values of the community, and then uses those values as the foundation of the plan. Second, it translates the values into an agreed-upon and preferred sense of place that can be used as the yardstick to measure the appropriateness of future development. Finally, it stimulates a sense of ownership for the plan, and ownership translates into support for implementation.

"[The city] is the product of many builders who are constantly modifying the structure for reasons of their own. While it may be stable in general outlines for some time, it is ever changing in detail. Only partial control can be exercised over its growth and form. There is no final result, only a continuous succession of phases."

—*Lynch* (1967, 2)

Participants at a pin-up session present their plans and discuss how well they performed against their own indicators. Visioning and Visualization Workshop cosponsored by the Lincoln Institute of Land Policy and the College of Architecture and Environmental Design at California Polytechnic State University at San Luis Obispo. (ACP–Visioning & Planning)

GIS information that is place-based, and emerging planning and PDDSS tools that enable communities and their citizens to track changes on how places are used and configured, can also play important roles in implementing a plan. They enable a shift from implementation through overly prescriptive regulations to a dynamic and responsive system in which demand (bottom-up) rather than supply (top-down) becomes the operative principle of implementation.

JUST-IN-TIME IMPLEMENTATION

Planners and architects have long prided themselves on their belief that they could create regulatory regimes that reflect with certainty how citizens will live, work, and recreate in the foreseeable future. The result has been highly prescriptive regulations that predetermine, on a lot-by-lot basis, where activities will happen and how intensive such activities will be. This approach to city design ignores the reality that cities are chaotic, unpredictable entities that are complex systems that manifest self-organizing and self-adjusting characteristics. If Lynch's observation from his book *The Image of the City* is true, as everyday experience tends to confirm, then the current practice of planning, designing, and regulating our cities is distinctly a nineteenth-century construct. It applies to the linear factory system of production in which cities are atomized into their component parts, optimized, and reassembled into a presumably rational whole.

Box 5.1 Managing Change Along Houston's Light Rail Corridor

Developed for the City of Houston by the Environmental Simulation Center, the Performance/Tracking/Allocation (P/T/A) System monitors growth along the city's recently completed Main Street light rail corridor. The goals were: (1) to measure the performance of the corridor against 22 community-based indicators; (2) to track change as it occurs and compare it with regional forecasts; and (3) to allocate future-year growth to where it is likely to occur. The P/T/A System consists of two components: the Land Development Model and the Performance Report Card.

The Land Development Model produces its monthly estimates of population, housing units, households, and employment by utilizing digital information already recorded by the City in the form of building permits. In the first example, the user can see the spatial distribution of building permits indicating higher than predicted housing activity and adjust the forecast accordingly (figure 5.1). The short feedback loop is extremely useful in targeting the planning and allocation of resources for infrastructure improvements to complement and encourage private investment. The second example illustrates the suitability of commercial development at a parcel level based on frontage on busy streets, proximity to light rail, lot size, and surrounding uses (figure 5.2).

Outputs from the Land Development Model "feed" the Performance Report Card, which allows the user to examine change for dozens of indicators (figure 5.3). The Performance Report Card organizes and evaluates the corridor's performance against expectations at multiple levels of geography—the entire corridor, any district, or any light rail station. Because the districts through which the light rail runs are quite diverse, each district may weight the indicators differently based on community values. Both the Land Development Model and Performance Report Card are transparent and user-adjustable.

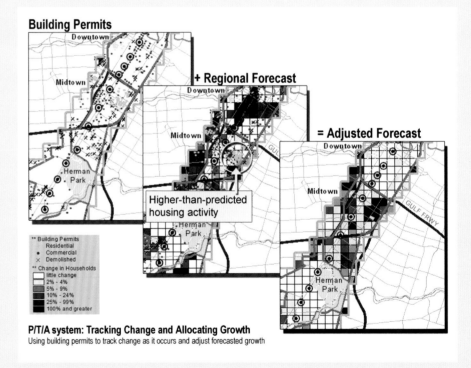

P/T/A system: Tracking Change and Allocating Growth
Using building permits to track change as it occurs and adjust forecasted growth

Figure 5.1 – Actual building permits collected on a monthly basis (green and red dots) are compared to the longer-term regional forecast of growth, as indicated by the grid in shades of blue. The data are then combined to created an "adjusted forecast" that takes into account what is actually happening on the ground. (Environmental Simulation Center, 2004)

More recently, planning, design, and regulatory approaches have emerged that are decidedly more indicative of twenty-first-century thinking. They are dynamic, embrace complexity, and respond to the flows of available information in iterative ways. The dynamism and complexity of the contemporary city argues for a method of planning, design, and regulation that is "just in time" rather than "not in time" (reactive) and "just in case" (overly proactive).

Just in time is a reference to Toyota's production philosophy of making only "what is needed, when it is needed, and in the amount needed." When translated into the implementation of a plan, just in time implies the existence of a highly sensitive system where citizens, elected officials, and urban professionals can closely monitor change and provide the necessary adjustments that facilitate implementation of a plan. The key to just-in-time planning is timely information provided through repeated feedback loops of the type that a GIS-based PDDSS can provide (box 5.1).

Just-in-time planning also implies a regulatory system that encourages creativity—the good you can't think of—by framing the problem rather than prescribing the solution. The GIS-based PDDSS discussed above can be adapted to support a just-in-time performance-based planning, design, and regulatory regime (boxes 5.2 and 5.3).

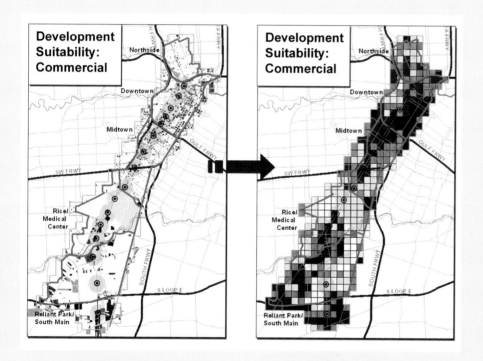

Figure 5.2 – Suitability of commercial land for development is parcel-based (left) and depends on frontage on busy streets, proximity to light rail, lot size, surrounding uses, and local lot-specific knowledge. This information can be used to create a simple model that distributes future development. The results were aggregated to the same grid cells used by the regional forecast so the two sets of information could be compared. (Environmental Simulation Center, 2004)

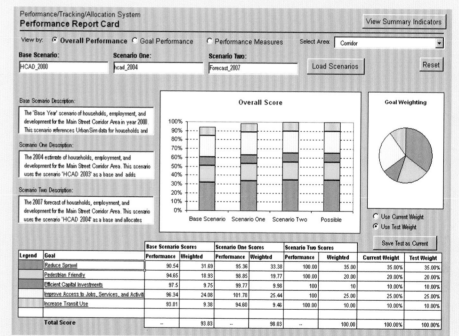

Figure 5.3 – A customized Microsoft Excel interface was created to sort, aggregate, graph, and compare dozens of performance indicators for up to three scenarios by multiple levels of geography. (Environmental Simulation Center, 2004)

Box 5.2 New York City's Housing Quality Zoning

The New York City Housing Quality Zoning Ordinance, adopted in 1976, was designed to recognize the uniqueness of the city's neighborhoods. It is a set of twenty-six guidelines or program elements divided into four categories: Neighborhood Impact, Security and Safety, Recreation Space, and Building Interior. Each program element contains a goal and a set of performance measures used to determine the degree of compliance with that goal. Rather than predetermining the appropriate building form, Housing Quality Zoning lays out the problem to be solved. Because it assumes that every situation has more than one "right" answer, trade-offs among program elements are built into the system. Partial compliance, measured as a percentage, receives a point score that is less than the maximum.

For example, the Neighborhood Impact section is essentially an urban design analysis (using GIS) of the development's immediate context that provides the values used in the performance measures. As a result, Housing Quality Zoning self-adopts to any situation and context. Housing Quality Zoning quickly and objectively establishes the degree of a building's compliance with clearly stated planning and design objectives (figures 5.4–5.7). It permits the architect or developer to choose which quality components to emphasize, as dictated by unique conditions such as marketing, neighborhoods, or sites.

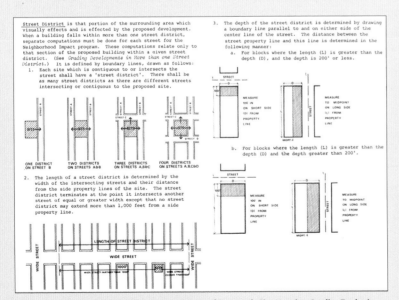

Figure 5.4 – Street district. (All images courtesy of New York City Housing Quality Zoning)

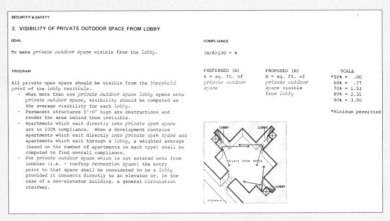

Figure – 5.5 Courtyards

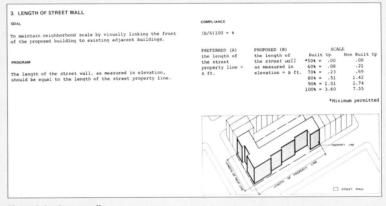

Figure 5.6 – Street wall

Figure 5.7 – Street wall height

Visioning and Visualization

Box 5.3 **New York City's Midtown Zoning**

In 1980 the chairman of the City Planning Commission in New York created a special task force to reevaluate the zoning regulations for Midtown, which had been in place since 1961. The task force's main goal was to review the environmental impact produced by the discretionary review process—especially as it concerned the amount of available daylight to streets, parks, plazas, and task lighting for office buildings—and propose as-of-right zoning regulations that would substitute for the uncertainties associated with discretionary zoning.

Midtown Zoning is an as-of-right performance system of as-of-right zoning based on objective criteria and measurement techniques that substitute for the outdated prescriptive height and setback regulations. The centerpiece of the new building bulk regulations is a modified Waldram diagram on which the daylighting performance of a building is evaluated against a threshold and standard (figure 5.8). The threshold and standard were systematically derived from an analysis of buildings and city blocks, developing a daylight map of Midtown Manhattan illustrating the sixty-year historical expectation of daylight in Midtown (figure 5.9).

Unlike standard prescriptive zoning that results in the ubiquitous tower-in-the-plaza, the Midtown regulation did not legislate a preferred building form, but rather set a performance standard to be achieved. The special midtown district zoning regulations were adopted into the New York City Zoning Ordinance in 1981 and are an acknowledged success.

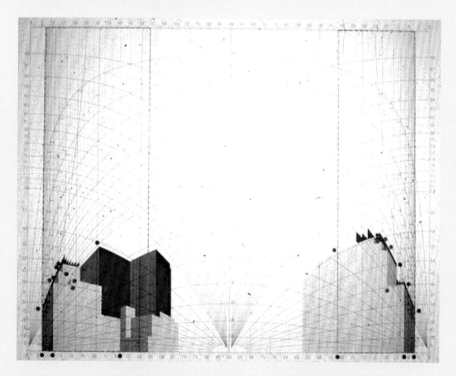

Figure 5.8 – The modified Waldram diagram used to evaluate daylighting for Midtown Zoning. (Image courtesy of Bowery Savings Bank Project, Skidmore, Owings, & Merrill, LLP)

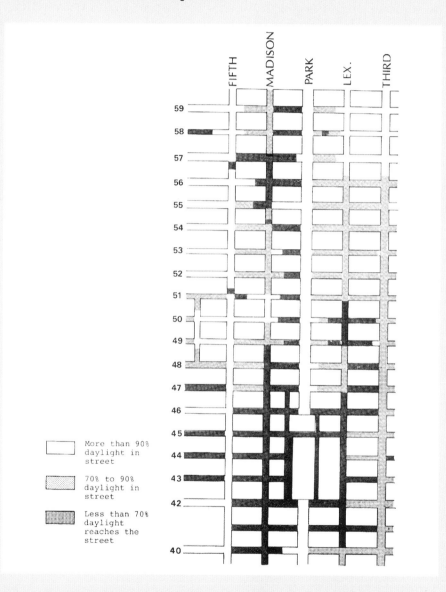

Figure 5.9 – Daylight map, from white areas with 90 percent daylight in streets to dark-gray areas, which have less than 70 percent daylight. (Image courtesy of Kwartler/Jones Architects, Planners, and Urban Design)

Unlike conventional planning and regulation, which is episodic (e.g., the plan and regulations are done once every x years, and then take on a kind of mosaic, immutable quality), PDDSS applications can be fully integrated into the public decision-making process to create scenarios, evaluate alternatives, and provide the basis for informed public discussion and decision making. In communities or even neighborhoods it is not unusual for the aggregates of incremental decisions, made over time, to lead to unintended and often unwanted consequences. Further, PDDSS tools provide the public environment in which to calibrate values and, when necessary, reevaluate their relevance and relative and absolute importance based on feedback from prior decisions and actions.

Unlike static systems, this new planning, design, and regulatory paradigm "learns" from experience and provides the means to be self-organizing and self-adjusting, often resulting in a "good" that could not have been anticipated in a top-down system. Representative of this is the process in which nineteenth-century industrial lofts in Manhattan, after years of illegal conversions, were repositioned to live-work spaces and finally to highly desirable dwelling units. Facilitated by the fact that loft buildings are underdetermined and "loose fit," builders experimented with ways to adapt the lofts to the needs of living and working, resulting in group learning that ultimately led to their legalization.

DEVOLVING DECISION MAKING IN IMPLEMENTATION

The tools described in chapter 4 enhance the potential to decentralize decision making to become the responsibility of those most familiar with the place, the issues, and the information needed to adjust decision making to local conditions. Thus, devolving decision-making powers in the implementation of a plan is critical to building social capital through a reinvigorated concept of citizenship, and it rejects the one-size-fits-all approach to planning, design, and regulation.

The devolution of control in implementation to the local level also creates the ideal environment for creativity and democratic decision making based on inclusion and enlightened understanding, control of the agenda, effective participation, and voting equality at the decisive stage—the key characteristics of a public involvement process, as described in chapter 2. The participation of community leaders and the excitement and good will of residents created by a rigorous public involvement process can continue in the implementation.

The follow-up and implementation phase of a public involvement process, however, is less-charted territory than operating within the formal government structure. Local issues and priorities, past history, the degree of trust that exists among key players, and the makeup of special interest groups all play important roles in shaping an informal implementation structure.

Notwithstanding local differences, the preferred informal way to conduct implementation is to form working groups and task forces to deal with specific implementation topics. The composition of a task force typically reflects the forces that gravitate toward a given issue and should replicate the implementation dynamics that exist in the community. Groups at opposite ends of a spectrum should often be invited to join the same task force.

In this way, task forces can become laboratories where ideas and proposals are discussed and refined or microcosms in which options are tested and ultimately brought to fruition with the buy-in and support of a broad spectrum of interests. Furthermore, task forces can accomplish things outside what government can do. For example, they can raise funds from sources that are typically off limits to government, and they can bring together the expertise of government with that of the private and nonprofit sectors. This flexibility results in usable action plans to which responsible parties can commit, thus sustaining participation and involvement of the community well beyond the development of a plan.

A CAUTIONARY NOTE ON DUE PROCESS

When used in public decision making, visual simulation must meet a series of tests that reflect constitutional due process values. The tests may vary depending on both the context in which the decision is being made and the type of decision. Those that most directly affect an individual's use of her own property typically require a higher standard than those that are more general or policy-oriented. The former would include discretionary approval of a project by a planning commission, while the latter could be a vision plan that generally affects the use of property in policy terms and serves as a context for future regulatory actions.

Due process relates in part to the information for which the issue is deliberated and the decision is made. The standards for due process regarding land use and private property are reasonableness and its prior or extensive use in decision making and accepted best practice. Because visual simulation is a relatively new tool, virtually no standards are in place. Without a clearly articulated standard that assures that the information provided meets the reasonableness test to make a considered decision, what is meant by realism or accuracy may vary from situation to situation. For example, a 3D model used to simulate a practical zoning build-out in a large geographic area may be built to a different level of accuracy and realism than one used to evaluate the visibility of floors added to a landmark building as seen from the street.

Unlike architectural renderings, which the public and decision makers have come to view with a certain degree of skepticism, visual simulations that include movement through a photorealistic environment tend to be taken at face value, possibly because they are so close to film, look real, and hence must be real. The fact that these prepathed simulations may involve editing, cropping, and the control of the "camera lens," and therefore ultimately manipulate the viewer's experience, has not been subject to public scrutiny.

Due process also concerns how a decision is made. It includes public access to information, how that information is used and communicated during public hearings, and the capacity of the public and decision makers to interpret it. Visual simulation presents a number of issues that remain open to debate. In the often contentious, adversarial nature of our public review process, not only are conflicting ideas brought to the discussion by the proponents and opponents, but different visual simulations of the same locale are debated as well.

For example, without a 3D GIS with a 3D model of the city that is accessible at no cost or at a modest cost to those involved in the debate, evaluating alternatives in a comparison becomes exceedingly difficult. Further, without reasonably equal access to the underlying information (in this example the 3D model), the playing field is no longer level and becomes restricted to those who can afford to play.

SUMMARY

Implementation is an integral, if not critical, component of the vision plan and process if the community's vision is to be realized. Implementation should be done on two complementary and parallel tracks: the formal track that includes the adoption of regulations, such as zoning and capital improvement plans; and the informal track that employs task forces that adopt aspects of the vision plan for implementation.

The advances in information technology and its capacity for fast feedback loops suggest the possibility of rethinking the land use regulatory structure— for example, moving from static, predetermined zoning regulations to a development code that is dynamic, just-in-time, and capable of tracking change and evaluating changes against performance indicators, suggesting a management versus regulatory approach to guided change.

The informal task forces suggest other implementation opportunities, including the raising of funds that may be difficult for a municipality, as well as the ability to become laboratories for innovation. Of equal importance, task forces may become the vehicle that sustains the participation and involvement of the community beyond the formulation of the vision plan.

6. Case Studies

The four case studies in this chapter describe how the public involvement techniques and 3D GIS-based simulation and visualization tools described in the previous chapters have been integrated and applied to address specific planning problems at the neighborhood, city, and regional scales. Each of these projects was conducted between 2001 and 2006 by ACP–Visioning & Planning and Environmental Simulation Center (ESC).

- Southwest Santa Fe City/County Master Planning Initiative for the City and County of Santa Fe, New Mexico

- Near Northside Economic Revitalization Planning Process for the City of Houston, Texas

- Kona Community Development Plan for the County of Hawaii, Hawaii

- Vision 2030: Shaping our Region's Future Together, a five-county vision developed for the Baltimore (Maryland) Regional Transportation Board

Each case deals with particular planning challenges and differing governmental and regulatory structures while utilizing a variety of public involvement settings, from small hands-on workshops to large town-hall meetings. In all of these case studies, public involvement and simulation and visualization techniques are applied at the outset of the planning process as tools to help the public make informed decisions. While each case is unique, there are strong commonalities that show why, how, and under what circumstances the integration of public involvement with simulation and visualization can enhance decision making.

Place plays a critical role in all four case studies. The ability to simulate and visualize physical conditions enables participants in the public process to experience the reality of their neighborhoods, cities, and regions in their most positive and negative aspects, rather than through the filter of abstract planning categories. The use of simulated and visualized conditions transforms planning and design into a form of inquiry. The public and the experts together discover and elaborate on the real-life implications of what is being proposed.

In a Mapping the Future Workshop for the Kona (Hawaii) Community Development Plan, participants simulated the process of land consumption and growth by placing chips where they wanted future development to occur. (ACP–Visioning & Planning)

SOUTHWEST SANTA FE CITY/COUNTY MASTER PLANNING INITIATIVE

The purpose of this study was to develop a vision for Southwest Santa Fe as a first step in creating a master plan for the area (with corresponding development regulations) that would implement the policy framework established by the vision. The territory of the plan area falls within both city and county jurisdictions. Southwest Santa Fe is subdivided into three areas: the Cerrillos/Airport/Rodeo Intersection, the Agua Fria area, and Airport Road. Over the next twenty years, Southwest Santa Fe, an area of 5,140 acres, is expected to reach a population of nearly 20,000, doubling the current number of residents.

The Southwest Santa Fe City/County Master Planning Initiative was a response to many issues affecting the region, including the speed of urbanization, inconsistent and permissive zoning, traffic congestion, loss of open space, and fears that current levels of water consumption were unsustainable. Ultimately, the goal of the process was to determine what type of place Southwest Santa Fe should become—whether it should continue to develop as an auto-dependent "suburb" of anonymous strip malls and gated communities in the adobe style, or whether it should grow in a way that would resonate with Santa Fe's historic development patterns, consider the values of the existing population, and conserve the high desert landscape. Hence, the focus of the public participation process was on the character of future growth.

Methodology/Process

The process, which was designed to identify a vision for Southwest Santa Fe, consisted of three sequential steps, each of which involved public participation, review, comment, and decision making.

1. Identify three prototypical areas where principles and possible development scenarios could be developed and applied.

2. Develop land use and urban design alternatives, including (a) identifying local patterns and conventions of development; (b) translating those patterns and conventions into the development of 3D building blocks; (c) extracting development principles from the building blocks; and (d) applying the building blocks to each of the three prototypical areas.

3. Test the land use and urban design alternatives with the vision's task force and present them to residents and stakeholders.

Three subareas within the larger project area were selected as representative of three prototypical conditions designated as new development, corridor development, and rural development. Next, recurring patterns of development were identified and translated into development building blocks. To a great extent, places derive their character from urban design conventions, or from recurring patterns implicitly agreed upon by the community. Examples of such patterns include the diversity of fences and walls that enclose the front yards of Santa Fe's houses or the generally uniform setbacks of houses in New England. Fifteen large and small recurring patterns used to design the building blocks in this case study were derived from historic Santa Fe and from the Southwest neighborhood itself.

Then, these local patterns were translated into digital 3D building blocks (blocks and lots consisting of houses, sidewalks, street widths, and on-street parking), which became the basic components used in developing the vision for each of the prototypical areas. A draft of the 3D building blocks was presented to the task force to review both individually and as aggregated patterns in the real-time 3D model.

The hierarchy of new streets and block sizes was reviewed in its entirety and as individual components; each street's width, design speed, sidewalks, and on-street parking patterns were explored. Each street type, from alley to collector street, was modeled in 3D using the building blocks based on historic street widths in Santa Fe. The Santa Fe Department of Transportation's standard street widths were also modeled for comparison (figure 6.1).

As the planning process proceeded, the individual building blocks were aggregated into development scenarios that were then applied to the prototypical areas using a GIS-based existing-conditions 3D model of the three prototypical areas. This process showed how the building blocks might be combined to create a neighborhood, a mixed-use commercial area, or a development pattern in low-density rural protection areas.

Fitting the building blocks and land use patterns to existing conditions demonstrated how the areas could develop incrementally and inclusively. The simulations and 3D visualizations were not intended to be finished, static designs rigidly applied, but rather illustrations of how the building blocks might be organized to show a possible, but by no means singular, end result.

Neighborhood Street Type A

Type A — Alternative 2

Characteristics:

Right of Way: 33'

Pavement: 24'

Design Speed: 30 / 35 mph

Traffic: one way

Sidewalks: 4' on two sides

Parking: two sides continuous

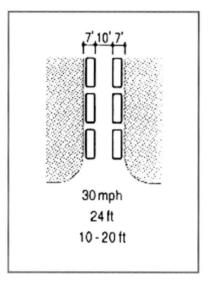

Neighborhood Street Type B

Type B — Alternative 2

Characteristics:

Right of Way: 28'

Pavement: 20'

Design Speed: 30 / 35 mph

Traffic: one way

Sidewalks: 4' on two sides

Parking: two sides staggered

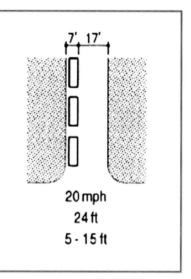

Figure 6.1 – A hierarchy of streets was modeled in real-time 3D for comparison purposes. On the left is a Santa Fe Department of Transportation standard 33' right-of-way for a one-way street and on the right is an alternative 28' right-of-way for a one-way street. The community was asked to vote on how comfortable they were overall with each street type taking into account issues of safety, traffic flow, environmental impact, and visual appeal. (Environmental Simulation Center, 2001)

Formulating the Development Principles

The results of the development scenario review by the steering committee were translated into ten development principles, each of which represented a basic core value agreed upon during the visioning process and listed the specific building blocks necessary to fulfill its intent. The principles generalized the results of the process, making the principles and the building blocks from which they were derived applicable throughout the entire planning area.

During the public meetings representative portions of each prototypical area were simulated at eye level and in real time to enable the participants to see what it would be like to walk, shop, and commute in each area (figure 6.2). This real-time walk-through was very effective in conveying the future identity of Southwest Santa Fe to the public. The 3D model also made it possible to respond to requests to walk down other streets, or to see the view from someone's front yard. Being able to be "in" the model and to make choices based on that experience was critical to engendering a spirited discussion of the pros and cons of the principles.

After considerable discussion, participants were asked to rank the principles on a scale ranging from 1 (indicating the lowest level of support) to 5 (the highest level), and an average score for each principle was tabulated. To increase public input, the designs and concept for Southwest Santa Fe were further reviewed and scrutinized through seven small-scale workshops with neighborhood associations and professional groups, and through a survey distributed to residents, business owners, students, and others throughout the planning area.

Discussing Density

Density was not discussed explicitly during the process. Rather than the abstraction of density numbers (e.g., dwelling units per acre), participants had an opportunity to evaluate the character of places and measure them against the principles they themselves had developed. In addition, the effects of density (or the lack thereof) on the consumption of land were demonstrated by the use of GIS-based dynamic maps and charts that graphically delineated the amount of land needed to meet the area's projected housing needs at three dwelling units per acre (existing zoning density), five dwelling units per acre, and eight dwelling units per acre—the density of Santa Fe's historic core (figure 6.3).

Figure 6.2 – Building blocks were compiled into real-time 3D models to simulate visually what Southwest Santa Fe might look like based on the community's principles. An aerial view (above) of a neighborhood, and eye-level views (opposite) show what a walk through the neighborhood might look like. (Environmental Simulation Center, 2001)

Conclusion

Through the visual simulations of the representative portions of each prototypical study and the land consumption demonstrations, it became clear that at current zoned densities all available land, including land fronting the Santa Fe River, would be developed, contradicting the desire to protect open space within the planning area. The GIS simulations and 3D visualizations enabled Southwest Santa Fe residents to agree to higher development densities, thus enabling the creation of more compact and walkable communities and allowing the preservation of open land on both sides of the river.

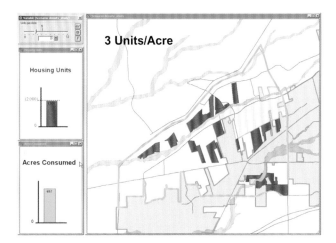

3 Units/Acre

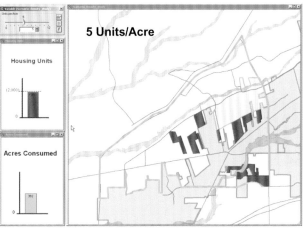

5 Units/Acre

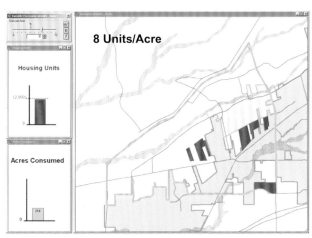

8 Units/Acre

Figure 6.3 – GIS analysis of land consumption in Southwest Santa Fe: The image at the top shows the amount of land that would be consumed at the current zoned density of 3 units/acre; the center image shows the preferred density of 5 units/acre; and the density of Santa Fe's historic core, 8 units/acre, is shown at the bottom. (Environmental Simulation Center, 2001)

HOUSTON'S NEAR NORTHSIDE ECONOMIC REVITALIZATION PLAN

The Near Northside Economic Revitalization Plan was an initiative of the City of Houston with grants from the U.S. Department of Housing and Urban Development (HUD) and the Federal Highway Administration (FHWA) Main Street Revitalization Project, with contributions from Avenue Community Development Corporation. The purpose of the plan was to develop a community-based vision for the neighborhood with a focus on its commercial corridor.

The Near Northside, located adjacent to Houston's downtown, is a predominantly Latino yet diverse neighborhood and was one of two city neighborhoods selected for HUD's Community Technology Initiative in 2001. A primary objective of the initiative was to demonstrate the role of visual simulation in helping communities collaboratively plan and reach consensus. The other objective was to make the initiative sustainable by training Houston's Planning and Development Department staff in the use of the new visualization simulation tools and how to apply them in future neighborhood visioning and planning workshops.

The Near Northside Economic Revitalization Plan was initiated to help the neighborhood benefit from its location adjacent to Houston's resurgent downtown. The proposed introduction of light rail also represented an extraordinary opportunity for the Near Northside neighborhood. The first phase of Houston's light-rail system now runs south to the first interstate ring road; the second phase is planned to pass through the Near Northside and terminate at the Bush International Airport.

The alignment of this light-rail line, and its potential positive impact linking Near Northside's commercial corridor with downtown, became one of the two focal points of the plan. The second was the fostering of a pedestrian-oriented, walkable neighborhood and shopping corridor in a city where development patterns were historically oriented toward the automobile. A significant portion of the public involvement process focused on urban design issues regarding future development in this commercial corridor.

Methodology/Process

The Near Northside case study demonstrates how visual simulation was ultimately instrumental in helping stakeholders understand their choices and reach consensus on a preferred future. It also demonstrates the pitfalls of a flawed planning process in which the Houston-based lead consultants did not appreciate the power of visual simulation to frame choices, foster discussion, and lead to consensus. As a result, the lead consultant failed to meaningfully integrate visual simulation into his design of the neighborhood planning process rather than as added "bells and whistles."

The most glaring example was the lead consultant's failure to introduce the concept of 3D real-time visual simulations—what they are and how they were going to be used to explore alternative corridor-development scenarios. Instead, the 3D realistic visual simulations of three possible development scenarios representing the upper and lower densities needed to support light rail, created by Environmental Simulation Center (ESC), were presented out of context and characterized as a "virtual reality tour" of future corridor development, similar to the kind of 3D animation used to sell condos. When confronted with these development scenarios in real-time, photorealistic 3D, the neighborhood participants were frustrated and outraged. Having to make the jump from discussing programs and policies to seeing the 3D visual simulation of development scenarios, none of which had been formulated by the participants, was a significant and jolting disconnect in the process.

Photorealistic 3D visual simulations, by necessity, involve making design decisions that reflect a shared value system and sense of community identity that had not been discussed with the Near Northside stakeholders. In the ensuing heated discussion, it became clear that the workshop participants assumed that the 3D walk-throughs were being used to sell the lead planning consultant's conclusions, rather than to inform the community-based decision-making process.

Moreover, ESC had envisioned that the simulation and visualization information would be used to stimulate an informed discussion at the beginning of the community visioning process. Because the simulations were shown after the process was well advanced, the community residents saw them as a product of a series of decisions in which they had had no role. The lesson to be learned is that, because simulations and visualizations appear to be real, when they are presented out of context, without a prior explanation of how they will be used in the community's planning process, stakeholders may take them literally, as faits accomplis, which subverts the public involvement process.

Revising the Methodology/Process

As a result of this confusion, ESC added another workshop to address five important issues.

1. Interpret the Near Northside community's perception of itself as it currently exists.

2. Help the community understand the rules of the game by visualizing the City of Houston's development regulations with a focus on parking requirements.

3. Reach agreement on the community's values and sense of its identity in both human and physical terms (where it is and where it wants to be).

4. Translate the community's values and sense of identity into a series of principles that would guide the way the Near Northside neighborhood would be developed.

5. Visually simulate those principles in three dimensions to ensure that what the community said is what it really meant.

In order to understand the community's perceptions of itself, its common values, and its sense of identity, this workshop began with a cognitive-mapping and narrative exercise that was designed to identify the community's positive and negative environmental images. Instead of using a formal questionnaire, which tends to channel the residents' responses, each participant was asked to describe his or her daily experience through both words and images. This approach was purposely open ended, leaving the length, format, and organization to the individual. Themes that had emerged in prior public meetings (e.g., walkability, pedestrian-friendly, shopping, housing, and landscaping) were mentioned in the instructions, but participants were not required to refer to them in their narratives or maps.

Principles to Guide Future Development

Interpretation of the narratives and maps showed that responses to the residential areas were generally positive, while impressions of daily shopping experiences were uniformly negative. The narratives revealed that residents usually went shopping on foot rather than by automobile, in part because of the Latino culture and economic situation. Most families have one car that is used for commuting to work in Houston's decentralized environment. As a result, walking to reach destinations within the Near Northside community is a way of life.

While the narratives identified many strong service and retail destinations, they were automobile-oriented and widely dispersed in the corridor, making them difficult to access on foot. The narratives noted the unpleasantness of negotiating curb cuts, parking lots, and discontinuous sidewalks, and the lack of shade from trees, pedestrian-oriented lighting for security, and places to sit while waiting for a bus. Implicit in the narratives was a desire to concentrate, connect, and create continuity among compatible activities. The goal of the workshop was to determine how these objectives could be formulated into principles, given physical form, agreed upon, and achieved.

ESC presented its interpretation of the stakeholder narratives and maps, and translated those results into a series of principles dealing with connectivity, continuity, and compatibility, which were also validated by the stakeholders. As a methodology for understanding residents' perceptions of their neighborhood, the narratives proved to offer, according to the participants, a nonthreatening and nonmanipulative means of inquiry.

Visualizing the Principles

The objective of this follow-up workshop was to reach consensus on how the previously articulated principles of connectivity, continuity, and compatibility would be achieved and could lead to the formulation of urban design guidelines to be adopted by the City of Houston. This approach was consistent with Houston's regulatory culture, which does not regulate use or density, but rather regulates site planning, landscaping and building configurations, and parking through urban design guidelines and a program of incentives.

To stimulate discussion, ESC prepared a photorealistic, real-time 3D digital model to simulate and visualize a range of development scenarios in the commercial and residential areas with and without the introduction of light rail. The 3D model was disaggregated into its constituent components (e.g., buildings, parking, streetscape) to create a set of building blocks that could be assembled and reassembled easily into alternative development scenarios.

The photorealistic 3D models used retail, office, restaurant, and housing types from Houston that were familiar to the participants. This use of vernacular buildings avoided the issue of architectural design quality and allowed the workshop to focus on urban design elements—the siting of buildings, the quality of the pedestrian experience, the configuration, usability, and accessibility of public open spaces, and the location of parking.

The use of the real-time simulation environment allowed ESC to simulate a pedestrian's experience of walking from a house to the commercial corridor. It also served to build confidence in the openness of the workshop process, since a participant could locate herself anywhere in the 3D model, rather than be limited to either static images or animations where the viewer's path and focus are predetermined. It was important that the participants saw the 3D digital model as support for decision making, rather than as a means to manipulate decision making.

Each of the principles was simulated and visualized as a set of either/or alternatives that contrasted a business-as-usual scheme (automobile-oriented with parking on the street, in front of buildings) with one that was pedestrian-oriented (parking lots behind or next to buildings). Each of the principles was presented in side-by-side comparisons with both eye-level and aerial views taken from the 3D model (figure 6.4a and b). The presentations also featured real-time walk-throughs that included a walk from a residential area to and along the commercial corridor, a walk to and ride on the light rail along the commercial corridor, and a driver's experience in the same area.

The side-by-side comparisons facilitated an informed discussion of the performance of each of the alternatives relative to the principles of connectivity, continuity, and compatibility, and an analysis of the alternatives relative to the degree to which they were auto-centric or pedestrian-centric (figure 6.5). As the workshop progressed, it became clear that, all other things being equal, the siting of buildings and parking lots favored either the driver or the pedestrian, and this became a fundamental choice on which the participants were asked to vote.

The final vote unanimously favored a neighborhood whose identity would be shaped by the pedestrian experience and its enhancement due to the insertion of light rail in the commercial corridor. Participants emphasized the power of 3D computer images of the neighborhood, both static and dynamic, to guide the discussion effectively and lead to consensus on a vision for the future that is consistent with the communities' values and identity.

Figure 6.4a – Eye-level view: "Apples-to-apples" comparison of parking in the front (above) to parking in the rear (below). The same buildings were used in each scenario, but arranged differently on the site. (Environmental Simulation Center, 2001)

Figure 6.4b – Aerial view showing the same buildings in two different scenarios: parking in rear (above) and parking in the front (below). (Environmental Simulation Center, 2001)

Figure 6.5 – Near Northside public workshop. (ACP–Visioning & Planning)

Formulating the Urban Design Guidelines and Technology Transfer

The next step was to translate the workshop results into urban design guidelines that were adopted by the city to implement in the Near Northside Plan. The final step was to transfer the visual simulation tools and methodology to Houston's Planning and Development Department's staff and preparation of a manual on how to use visual simulation in consensus-building community design workshops in other Houston neighborhoods as part of the city's Super Neighborhood Program.

Conclusion

In two fundamental ways, the use of 3D visual simulations greatly enhanced the public decision-making process and the building of community consensus when they were an integral part of the planning and visioning process. First, the visual simulations were used not to sell the plan or vision, but to inform its creation by the participants throughout the decision-making and consensus-building processes. Second, the simulations translated the abstractions of scenarios, public policies, and principles into 3D models that palpably represented the place(s) that would result from their implementation.

Unlike with maps and physical models, participants could put themselves inside the 3D digital models and walk through them at eye level, as well as query the underlying data. Moreover, the visual simulations were used iteratively, responding to participants' suggestions. The 3D models were quickly modified and new scenarios created, visually simulating policies and scenarios before they were implemented to ensure that, like Horton, "I meant what I said and I said what I meant" (Seuss 1954).

KONA COMMUNITY DEVELOPMENT PLAN

Kona is a district on the western coast of the Big Island of Hawaii. It is a popular tourist destination that has been experiencing robust growth, with a population increase from 29,942 residents in 1990 to approximately 41,940 in 2005 (an increase of 40 percent). However, population numbers tell only part of the story; growth in housing units provides a more realistic picture.

Between 1990 and 2000 the number of new housing units (many of them second homes) increased from 7,947 housing units in 1990 to 13,330 in 2000, an increase of more than 67 percent. This asymmetrical increase creates disproportionate land consumption and infrastructure needs and has contributed to community concerns about the loss of significant natural, cultural, and agricultural resources. The community has also experienced difficulty providing the infrastructure necessary to accommodate this growth.

The Kona Community Development Plan (CDP) was designed to translate the broad goals and policies of Hawaii County's General Plan, adopted in 2005, into specific actions and priorities for particular geographic areas in the districts of North and South Kona. The Kona CDP was the first to be enacted under the General Plan and is set up to be a model for future CDPs on the island.

ACP–Visioning & Planning designed the public process for the CDP and worked closely with ESC, which provided the technical analysis and visualizations used throughout the process. The results of each activity informed the content of succeeding ones to ensure that the public was involved in making all critical decisions for the CDP. Great emphasis was placed on visualizing options and on using images to engage the public in making informed choices. These methods were particularly important because a large part of the public process was dedicated to the issue of future growth of the community (figure 6.6).

Methodology/Process

The Kona CDP public involvement process consisted of four phases:

Gathering Ideas—to create the foundation of ideas upon which all subsequent activities were based;

Mapping the Future—to address critical questions and identify where future growth should occur;

How Do We Grow? Charrettes 1 and 2—to identify preferred development patterns; and

Working Groups—to identify objectives and actions for inclusion in the specific elements of the CDP.

Gathering Ideas   The idea-gathering phase consisted of two major activities: structured interviews and public meetings. In September 2005, the consultant team conducted a series of structured focus group interviews with a variety of stakeholder groups, including representatives from the tourism industry, the

Figure 6.6 – A visual simulation showing a Growth Opportunity Area alternative at 8 units per acre (net). (Environmental Simulation Center, 2006)

development community, business, large and small property owners, native Hawaiians, long-term residents, and newcomers. These interviews were structured to expose perceptions, attitudes, and critical issues faced by the Kona community.

To ensure balanced demographic and geographic participation of residents, 109 individual public meetings were held throughout Kona from November 2005 through January 2006. These meetings were offered "on-demand," and trained facilitators arranged to meet with interested parties to gather ideas using a prescribed format that involved general brainstorming and responses to critical questions. More than 800 residents generated the 3,496 ideas that were recorded and sorted into 18 categories. These categories were then used by the CDP Steering Committee to develop a set of goals that captured a desired outcome for the future of Kona. The categories were also used by the working groups as the material upon which to develop objectives and strategies for the elements of the CDP.

Mapping the Future   The second phase was designed to answer the question, where do we grow? This Mapping the Future Workshop, conducted in February 2006, was a four-hour activity attended by more than 350 residents organized into 32 facilitated groups.

The first part of the workshop was designed to address questions related to policy and implementation issues that had been raised by the structured interviews and ideas generated at the public meetings. Small groups were randomly assigned to address one of twelve topics: housing choice; housing affordability; agriculture; transportation and land use; congestion; parks, recreation, and open space; protection of the environment; hazard mitigation; protection of ancestral and historic sites; community character; retail; and tourism.

The second exercise initiated a dialog on regional character, cultural priorities, environmental protection issues, and preferred locations for future growth by asking participants about three issues:

1. Define criteria for the protection of ancestral and historic sites.

2. Define criteria for the protection of land for environmental and open space reasons.

3. Address the issue of land consumption in Kona.

Participants first considered and mapped historic sites and other geographic and environmental features that should be protected. Then they recommended appropriate locations where future growth could occur, based on cultural and geographic constraints and on land available within areas defined by the County General Plan as expansion areas. This Mapping the Future segment enabled participants to begin to deal with the issue of balancing future growth with the imperative of respecting ancestral cultural resources and protecting the unique environmental features of the Kona region. A variety of GIS-based maps provided technical background and informed the participants' discussion (figures 6.7 and 6.8).

The Mapping the Future exercise also involved an intuitive simulation of the process of land consumption and growth in Kona over the next 15 years. In this "game," participants, working in groups of 10, were given a number of chips, each representing an area of 40 acres. The total number of chips (139) represents the amount of land needed to accommodate expected population growth if current development trends were to continue (5,521 acres). This acreage was projected based on actual land consumption for the period 1995 to 2005, taking into account the continuing second-home phenomenon.

Participants were able to place chips in areas where they wanted future growth to occur. They could select unprotected, undeveloped lands, such as existing open space or agricultural lands, or they could select developed land areas, indicating a desire for redevelopment, infill development, or increasing intensity of development in existing communities. They could also indicate intensity of development by doubling or tripling chips in particular areas (figure 6.9).

The results of this simulation phase indicated strong consensus on a number of locations within the General Plan's designated Urban Expansion Area. These preferred Growth Opportunity Areas (GOAs) focused the majority of future development in the most urbanized area of North Kona, limiting development in South Kona to infill and redevelopment. All the maps generated by the public were digitized and integrated into the project's GIS to gain an understanding of the public's preferences. In an innovative use of GIS, these composite maps were used to analyze the degree to which there was consensus on both the location and intensity (degree of development compactness) of future development. Once agreement was reached on where future growth should occur, the focus of the public process shifted to how that development should occur.

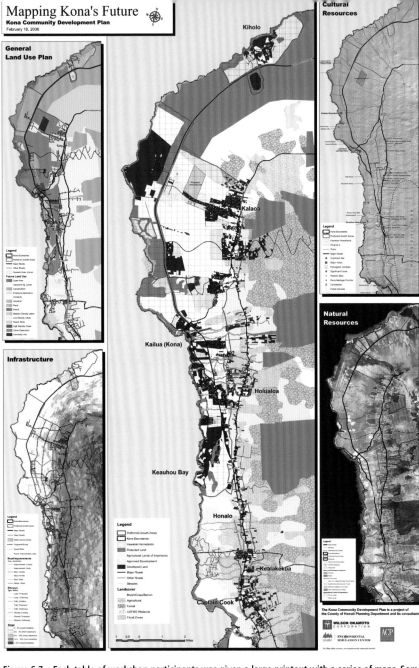

Figure 6.7 – Each table of workshop participants was given a large printout with a series of maps. Some tables were given maps for the entire 800-square-mile region, and they concentrated on rural issues. Other tables were given maps that focused on the county's preferred urban expansion area (pictured). The center map was the main working map and showed already developed or developing areas, roads, protected lands, and the county's preferred urban expansion areas. Four other thematic maps were provided for reference: the county's general land use plan; infrastructure; cultural resources; and natural resources. (Environmental Simulation Center, 2006)

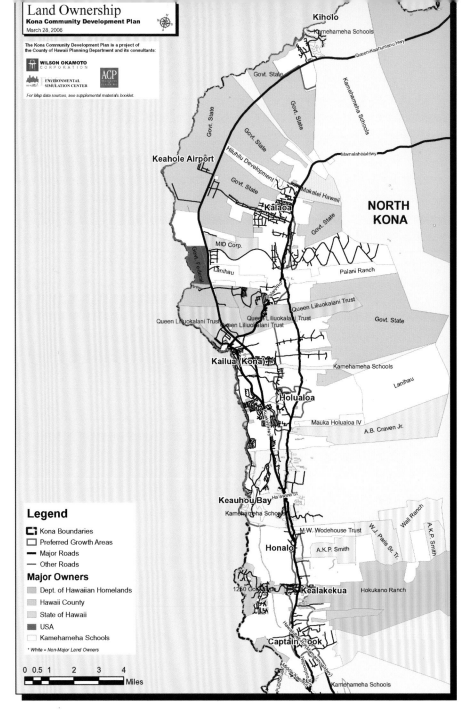

Figure 6.8 – A supplemental land ownership map was created and used during workshops. Large parts of the region are held by a few major landowners, including the Kamehameha Schools Trust, the Queen Liliuokalani Trust, and the State of Hawaii. (Environmental Simulation Center, 2006)

Visioning and Visualization

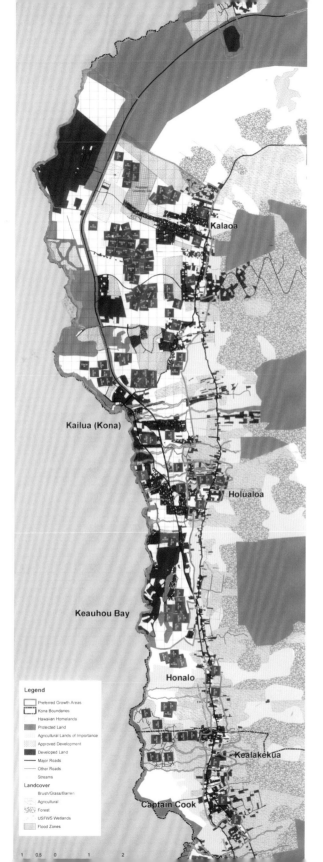

Figure 6.9 – A typical map produced by one group during Kona's Mapping the Future exercise. The red chips represent areas where those participants preferred to see growth. After the workshop, each group's map was scanned and entered into the GIS, thereby capturing the preferences of every participant and highlighting where there is consensus for growth. (Environmental Simulation Center, 2006)

How Do We Grow?—Charrettes 1 and 2 The third phase of Kona's public involvement process utilized two charrettes, in March and June 2006, to address development concepts and the nature and quality of future growth. Each charrette consisted of a variety of activities, including public meetings, open houses, and meetings with the Kona CDP Steering Committee.

To determine their relative importance, development principles based on public comments gathered during the Mapping the Future workshop were rated by participants in the first charrette. These principles would provide guidance for a range of activities throughout the CDP process, indicating community preferences related to the location and type of future development.

Participants were also asked to review the locations of previously designated GOAs on a large-scale map and to comment on their appropriateness, based on their knowledge of the terrain, information about existing and proposed roads, environmental constraints, and the relationship of selected areas to existing and proposed developments. The GOAs were further refined during the second charrette with additional input from the public.

The GOAs are areas where incentives should be used to stimulate development. Incentives could include expediting the permitting process, public transportation, specially tailored zoning regulations, and infrastructure provided by the county's bonding capacity for water supply, wastewater, districtwide drainage, and roads. A parallel set of disincentives could be developed for land outside the GOAs by promoting the retention of open spaces and working lands, adopting tools such as transfers of development rights to compensate landowners, or acquiring land inside the expansion areas for open space protection.

In the spirit of the CDP development principles and goals, the GOAs should be zoned for higher densities and mixed uses (including residential mixed uses) and density bonuses for affordable housing, and they should have form-based or performance zoning to ensure that density is created through quality design features. The GOAs provide an opportunity to rationalize the development context in Kona so that development happens in a coherent fashion, and through the creation of villages and neighborhoods as opposed to individual and disconnected subdivision development (figure 6.10).

During the first charrette, participants at the public meeting analyzed a series of four future development scenarios that simulated what would happen if future growth were to be accommodated at four different densities (figure 6.11).

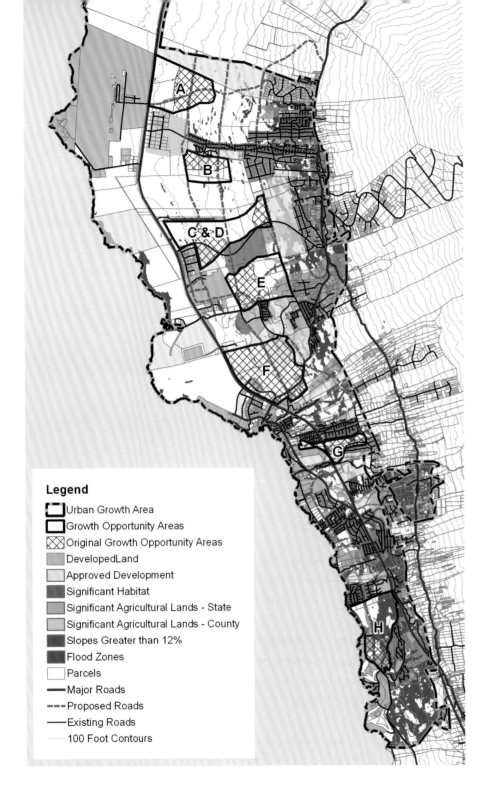

Responses to each of the scenarios indicated that the public's preferences were strongly in favor of higher-density scenarios, somewhere between scenarios C and D, with an average net residential density between five and eight net units per acre. This density was used to develop the preferred land use scenario and to inform visualizations of future development patterns.

A total of 17 visualizations (building blocks) were formulated to illustrate conditions likely to be created under the average five to eight net units per acre in the preferred scenario, and a continuum of conditions from neighborhoods to village centers. Visualizations also addressed residents' concerns about uniformity and scale. The building blocks were presented and rated during the second charrette (figure 6.12).

The results of the rating exercises indicated a preference for communities with well-defined centers, parking behind buildings, and a walkable and social environment. The participants also indicated a preference for neighborhoods that offer varied housing types, setbacks, and lots, while they expressed a dislike for conditions associated with conventional subdivision developments (e.g., uniform lots and housing sizes and lack of sidewalks). Based on these preferences, a prototypical GOA was created by assembling the building blocks (figures 6.13 and 6.14).

The responses to the building blocks provided critical information to be used in the development of regulatory tools to implement the compact neighborhoods and village vision expressed through the preferred development scenario. In addition, the building blocks were used by the CDP Steering Committee and county officials to analyze the physical implications of density bonuses in the range of 20 to 30 percent for the provision of affordable housing.

Working Groups   This final phase of the public process created a mechanism that allowed for citizen input in the policy-level phase of the CDP development over a period of about six months. A facilitator in each group helped guide the process. At a minimum, one member from the CDP committee was in each group to function as a liaison and keep the Steering Committee informed on the process.

Figure 6.10 – The Growth Opportunity Areas (GOAs, outlined in black) were created from the locational choices developed during the Mapping the Future exercise and further refined in subsequent workshops using a variety of constraints including areas of significant habitat and agricultural use, steep slopes, flood zones, and existing land ownership. Actual buildable land was calculated in the GIS to ensure that the GOAs were the correct size to accommodate the anticipated future growth. (Environmental Simulation Center, 2006)

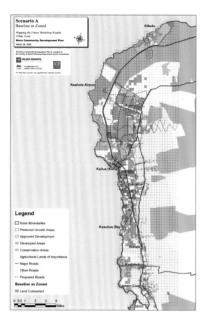

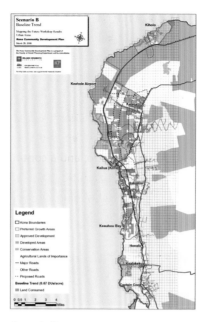

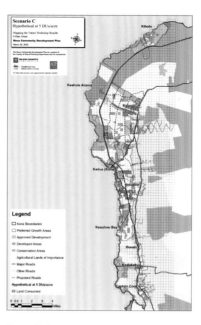

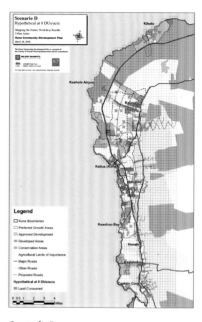

Scenario A

Development: distributed using current zoning densities

Additional Acres Needed: 9,265

Scenario B

Development: distributed at the average density of current trends

Additional Acres Needed: 1,492

Scenario C

Development: distributed at a density of five dwelling units per acre, which represents approximately the maximum density allowed under current zoning

Additional Acres Needed: 990

Scenario D

Development: distributed at eight dwelling units per acre

Additional Acres Needed: 661

Figure 6.11 – This series of maps shows land consumption in four scenarios. (Environmental Simulation Center, 2006)

A total of 12 groups addressed the following topics, which are somewhat different from the original set of 12 topics: agriculture, cultural resources, economy, energy, environment, facilities and programs, flooding and natural hazards, government, housing, land use and planning, recreation, and transportation. Drawing upon the input from each of the previous phases, the working groups identified specific objectives and actions to be included in the final CDP.

Conclusions

The vision set forth by the public and articulated in the Kona CDP document is multifaceted and complex, and it requires a profound rethinking of the way land will be used in the region in the future. The vision suggests a dramatic shift in emphasis from growth by disconnected and often gated subdivisions to the creation of integrated villages and neighborhoods. As visually simulated in a 3D model, a prototypical GOA is linked and walkable, and offers mixed uses and buildings of different types and costs. It calls for celebrating the native culture while respecting the ancestral places that are sacred, and for considering all aspects of the natural environment—from the *mauka* (ocean) to the *makai* (mountain) lands to agriculturally profitable areas and places for recreation. This vision will create a connected green infrastructure that defines and shapes the built environment.

This vision also demands a strong focus on affordable housing, not just as an issue of social equity but as a way to reduce congestion and workers' commuting

distance. It requires establishing a new rigorous set of development regulations to enable the implementation of the vision. And, finally, it will require innovative partnerships of private, public, and civic interests committed to implementing the vision over the long term.

The multifaceted vision expressed in the Kona CDP could not have been achieved without the use of visualizations that allowed the public to work directly with technical information and visualize the outcome of a variety of future scenarios. The melding of the intuitive knowledge brought to the table by the public and the technical analysis contributed by the consultant team ensured that the participants made informed and technically sound decisions while pursuing a vision for the region consistent with their values and expectations.

Figure 6.12 – A visual simulation of a pedestrian-oriented village center building block with parking predominately behind the buildings. (Environmental Simulation Center, 2006)

Figure 6.13 – A visual simulation of a conventional subdivision development with uniform housing sizes, types, and setbacks. This typical development type includes front-loaded garages and numerous curb cuts. (Environmental Simulation Center, 2006)

Figure 6.14 – A visual simulation showing a variety of housing types, sizes, and setbacks. Garages and small ohana houses (flats for extended family) are in the rear yards and are accessed via alleys and pathways. (Environmental Simulation Center, 2006)

Visioning and Visualization

BALTIMORE'S VISION 2030: SHAPING THE REGION'S FUTURE TOGETHER

Vision 2030: Shaping the Region's Future Together was an initiative of the Baltimore Regional Transportation Board with the support of the Baltimore Metropolitan Council and the Baltimore Regional Partnership. This initiative was designed to create a broad and clear vision for the future of the Baltimore region, and to help understand how best to shape mobility and growth in the region. The Baltimore region, with a population of more than 2,500,000 residents, includes the cities of Annapolis and Baltimore and the counties of Anne Arundel, Baltimore, Carroll, Harford, and Howard. The vision process was a response to a number of issues affecting the region.

- In 2000, while the region's population was growing, it was doing so unevenly. Newer suburbs were gaining population while Baltimore City and older suburban areas were losing it. New development was occurring at very low density, eroding the economic strength of the urbanized core, and changing the character of the region.

- The region was in the federal category of severe nonattainment quality standards.

- Baltimore City had 57.5 percent of its population living in poverty, and poverty was also increasing in older suburban communities. Lack of affordable housing and a disconnect between jobs, public transportation, and affordable housing was exacerbating the problem.

- Vehicle miles traveled were increasing at a rate five times faster than the rate of population growth for the region, raising congestion levels.

In response to these issues, over a 15-month period Vision 2030 explored six thematic areas revealed by a public process: economic development, education, environment, government and public policy, livable communities (growth and equity issues), and transportation. These themes were brought together for the first time to form a comprehensive and coherent regional perspective.

An extensive series of stakeholder interviews and three focus groups with randomly selected inner-city, suburban, and rural residents revealed the magnitude of concerns about the way growth was occurring and the inequity that it was creating. The results of the interviews and focus groups supported the greater emphasis given to growth and equity issues within the process and legitimized the exploration of issues generally considered the domain of local governments, such as where future growth should occur, and its nature and character.

Methodology

This case study focuses exclusively on the methodology used to integrate the design of the public process with the use of visualizations and simulations. The process was driven by three simple questions:

- What land within the region should be protected from development, and why?

- Where should development be encouraged, and why?

- How should future development occur?

The regional Where Do We Grow? workshop addressed the first two questions. It attracted elected officials, planners, educators, citizen activists, staff from NGOs, and business leaders, all of whom were separated into small, facilitated groups. Each group used a GIS-generated map of the region that included layers delineating urbanized areas, areas already protected from future development, agricultural areas, and unprotected farms and wetlands (figure 6.15). The maps used a one-square-mile (640 acre) grid to facilitate the group process.

Each group first made recommendations on the criteria (e.g., creation of contiguous natural environments, protecting forest and trail areas) and quantity of land to protect from future development. Then, using colored chips, each representing one square mile of land, they made recommendations for where land protection would be most appropriate. Each group compared and presented their proposed placement of chips. The discussion revealed an underlying consistency in the choices made by each group.

The next step in the regional workshop process was to determine the preferred locations for future growth. The groups received red chips that represented, at the same scale as the map, the amount of land needed to accommodate the region's projected growth for the next 25 years (figure 6.16). The calculation assumed that current development patterns and trends would continue.

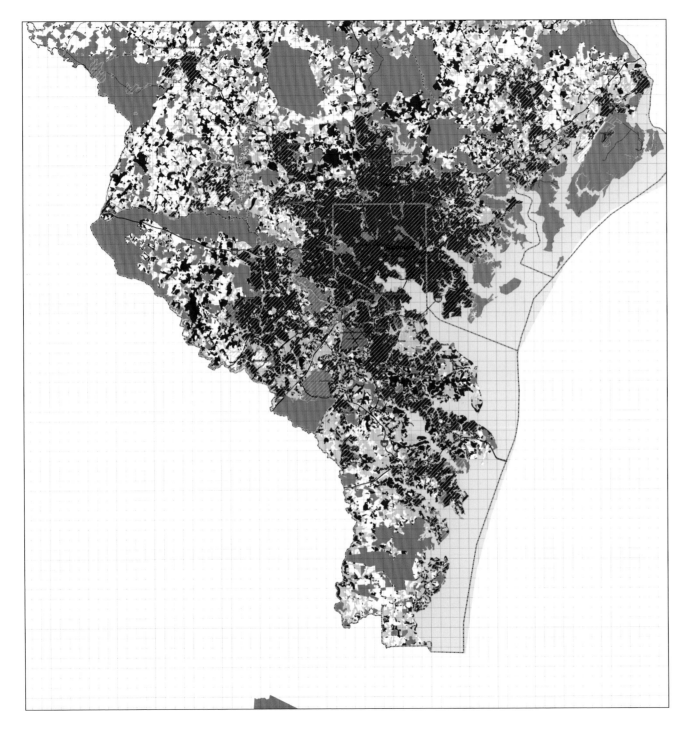

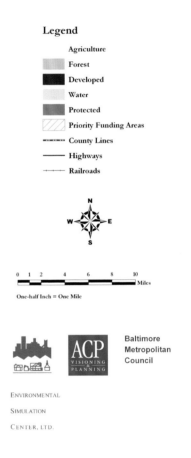

The
Baltimore Region
Regional Workshop
October 3, 2001

Legend

Agriculture

Forest

Developed

Water

Protected

//// Priority Funding Areas

╌╌╌ County Lines

── Highways

─┼─ Railroads

0 1 2   4   6   8   10
Miles

One-half Inch = One Mile

VISIONING & PLANNING

ACP

Baltimore
Metropolitan
Council

ENVIRONMENTAL
SIMULATION
CENTER, LTD.

Figure 6.15 – The regional map produced for the Where Do
We Grow? exercise shows Baltimore and its surrounding
counties. The number of elements used on the map was kept
to a minimum, providing enough information to complete the
exercise without overwhelming participants with too many
variables. (Environmental Simulation Center, 2002)

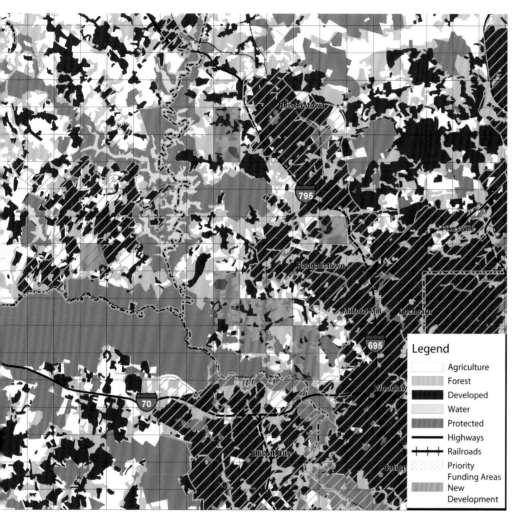

Legend

- Agriculture
- Forest
- Developed
- Water
- Protected
- Highways
- +++ Railroads
- Priority Funding Areas
- New Development

Figure 6.16 – A close up of a typical Where Do We Grow? map showing the 640-acre grid and some chips representing the workshop participants' locational choices for future growth in the Baltimore area. (Environmental Simulation Center, 2002)

Participants discussed and agreed on criteria for allocating future growth (e.g., along transit lines in already developed areas, in undeveloped areas, near employment centers). Once tabulated and discussed, the results revealed a strong emphasis on redevelopment rather than new development.

Results

The Vision 2030 Oversight Committee (a diverse group of 36 civic leaders) and four ad hoc citizen committees used the workshop results to identify and articulate development principles for the region, and to agree on three prototypical development patterns and four scenarios to be presented to the public for review and validation.

Over a two-month period, 17 facilitated regional public meetings were held to explore how the region should grow. These meetings had a dual function. First, they offered an opportunity for participants to brainstorm unconstrained ideas about the future of the region. Education, economic development, environmental factors, and social concerns topped the list of the issues that surfaced through the brainstorming. Second, the public provided additional feedback on proposed prototypical development patterns and regional development scenarios. The three development patterns reflected representative development trends in the Baltimore region and nationally. Each offered different implications for the consumption of land, mix of housing types, and proximity to jobs, shopping, and entertainment (figure 6.17a–c).

Each prototypical development pattern had the same goal that allowed for consistent comparisons: to accommodate one thousand households while supporting commercial areas, schools, and open space. Prototypical building types were modeled in three dimensions to reflect the character of buildings in the region. The 3D GIS environments were organized in real-time, walk-through paths to be presented to the public at the regional public meetings.

The 3D simulations and visualizations of the three development patterns were then used to assemble the four hypothetical regional development scenarios that accommodated the forecasted population and employment growth for the region by using the development patterns in different quantitative combinations (figure 6.18).

Scenario 1 focused on current trends and plans. It assumed that 90 percent of the growth would continue in the form of conventional development, with more compact communities on undeveloped and redeveloped land, each accounting for 5 percent of future growth.

Figure 6.17a – *Pattern 1:* This conventional development pattern, reflecting a continuation of existing regional growth trends, assumed use of undeveloped land. (Environmental Simulation Center, 2002)

Figure 6.17b – *Pattern 2:* A more compact, mixed-use community, also assumed to occur on undeveloped land, included a mix of housing types and the integrated shopping, entertainment, and employment functions. (Environmental Simulation Center, 2002)

Scenario 2 assumed that transportation investments would focus on increasing the region's road capacity. It accommodated 75 percent of future growth in conventional development, with more compact development patterns on new land and on redeveloped land set respectively at 20 and 5 percent.

Scenario 3 assumed that transportation investments would emphasize mass transit. It accommodated 25 percent of future growth in conventional development, with more compact development patterns on new land and on redeveloped land at 35 percent each.

Scenario 4 assumed that policies in the region would favor redevelopment; it accommodated 60 percent of future growth in redevelopment areas, with conventional and more compact development patterns on new land at 20 percent each.

The most obvious difference among the scenarios was the way they consumed land (138,316 acres in Scenario 1 versus 41,243 acres in Scenario 4). Beyond that, the regional impact of each scenario was measured through a complex computer model developed by Smart Mobility. The 3D GIS simulations and visualizations of the development patterns were used to provide the data in the model.

The three development patterns, the four regional development scenarios, and the performance measures were presented and tested at each of the 17 regional public meetings. These simulations and visualizations and the performance measures from the computer model provided participants with compelling visual and quantitative information from which to make their choices. The results demonstrated overwhelming support for Scenario 3, with its emphasis on mass transit, and Scenario 4, with its emphasis on redevelopment.

Figure 6.17c – *Pattern 3:* This even more compact, mixed-use community was assumed to occur on redeveloped land. (Environmental Simulation Center, 2006)

Figure 6.18 – An eye-level view of the village center in a compact, mixed-use community *(Pattern 2).* (Environmental Simulation Center, 2002)

Conclusions

The visualizations and simulations developed for Vision 2030 were a critical component in the process of enabling the public to make informed decisions for the future of the Baltimore region. Although regional issues are notoriously difficult to grasp in layperson's terms, the visualizations and computer modeling enabled participants to understand clearly the qualitative and quantitative implications of their choices. Upon completion of the visioning process, a telephone survey conducted on a random sample of 1,200 residents further validated the results of the vision process.

References

Alexander, Christopher. 1966. *Notes on the synthesis of form.* Cambridge, MA: Harvard University Press.

Alexander, Christopher, Sara Ishikawa, and Murray Silverstein. 1977. *A pattern language: Towns, buildings, construction.* New York: Oxford University Press.

Antenucci, John C., Kay Brown, Peter Croswell, and Michael J. Kevany. 1991. *Geographic information systems: A guide to the technology.* New York: Van Nostrand Reinhold.

Arnheim, Rudolf. 1977. *The dynamics of architectural form.* Berkeley: University of California Press.

Bosselman, Peter. 1998. *Representation of places: Reality and realism in city design.* Berkeley: University of California Press.

Brail, Richard K., and Richard E. Klosterman, eds. 2001. *Planning support systems: Integrating geographic information systems, models, and visualization tools.* Redlands, CA: ESRI Press.

Dahl, Robert A. 1989. *Democracy and its critics.* New Haven, CT: Yale University Press.

Gibson, James J. 1986. *The ecological approach to visual perception.* Hillsdale, NJ: Lawrence Erlbaum Associates.

Gombrich, E.H. 1980. Standards of truth: The arrested image and the moving eye. In *The language of images,* W.J.T. Mitchell, ed. Chicago: University of Chicago Press.

———. 2000. *Art and illusion:* Princeton, NJ: Princeton University Press.

Hagen, Margaret A., ed. 1980. *The perception of pictures.* Vol. 1: *Alberti's window: The projective model of pictorial information.* New York: Academic Press.

Heckscher, August. 1977. *Open spaces: The life of American cities.* New York: Harper & Row.

Jacobs, Jane. 1993. *The death and life of great American cities:* New York: Modern Library.

Kemmis, Daniel. 1990. *Community and the politics of place:* Norman, OK: University of Oklahoma Press.

Krampen, Martin. 1979. *Meaning in the urban environment.* London: Pion.

Lynch, Kevin. 1967. *The image of the city.* 3rd ed. Cambridge, MA: MIT Press.

———. 1976. *Managing the sense of a region.* Cambridge, MA: MIT Press.

———. 1981. *A theory of good urban form.* Cambridge, MA: MIT Press.

Maantay, Juliana, and John Ziegler. 2006. *GIS for the urban environment.* Redlands, CA: ESRI Press.

McHarg, Ian. 1969. *Design with nature.* Garden City, NY: Natural History Press.

McLuhan, Marshall. 1967. *The medium is the massage: An inventory of effects.* New York: Bantam

Mitchell, W.J.T., ed. 1980. *The language of images.* Chicago: University of Chicago Press.

New York Times. 1995. Excerpts from [Senator Bill] Bradley's speech to the Press Club. February 10.

Portugali, Juval. 1999. *Self-organization and the city:* Berlin: Springer.

———. 2005. *The construction of cognitive maps.* Berlin: Springer.

———. 2006. *Complex artificial environments: Simulation, cognition and virtual reality in the study and planning of cities.* Berlin: Springer.

Seuss, Dr. 1954. *Horton hatches the egg.* New York: Random House.

Sinclair, Upton. 2004. *The jungle.* New York: Pocket Books.

Zeisel, John. 1981. *Inquiry by design: Tools for environment-behavior research.* Monterey, CA: Brooks/Cole.

Index

About the Authors

Michael Kwartler, FAIA

Michael Kwartler, an architect, planner, urban designer, and educator, is the founding director of the Environmental Simulation Center (ESC), a nonprofit research laboratory in New York City created to develop innovative applications of information technology for community planning, design, and decision making. He conceived and directed the design and development of CommunityViz™, the first GIS-based planning decision support software to fully integrate virtual reality with scenario design, impact analysis, and policy simulation. With funding from the Ford Foundation, he is currently directing the development and deployment of a new multidimensional information technology tool for multiple stakeholders that integrates physical and human development within rapidly changing neighborhoods.

Gianni Longo

Gianni Longo is an architect and founding principal of ACP–Visioning & Planning in New York City. For more than two decades he has pioneered the development of programs designed to involve citizens in the decision-making process. He conceived and developed Vision 2000, a program of community goal setting in Chattanooga, Tennessee. Recently he designed the creative public involvement strategies for Imagine New York: Giving Voice to the People's Visions, an award-winning effort to bring together people throughout the New York metropolitan region to share their ideas and vision for rebuilding downtown and memorializing the World Trade Center tragedy.

About the Lincoln Institute of Land Policy

The Lincoln Institute of Land Policy is a private operating foundation whose mission is to improve the quality of public debate and decisions in the areas of land policy and land-related taxation in the United States and around the world. The Institute's goals are to integrate theory and practice to better shape land policy and to provide a nonpartisan forum for discussion of the multidisciplinary forces that influence public policy. This focus on land derives from the Institute's founding objective—to address the links between land policy and social and economic progress—that was identified and analyzed by political economist and author Henry George.

The work of the Institute is organized in four departments: Valuation and Taxation, Planning and Urban Form, Economic and Community Development, and International Studies. We seek to inform decision making through education, research, demonstration projects, and the dissemination of information through publications, our Web site, and other media. Our programs bring together scholars, practitioners, public officials, policy advisers, and involved citizens in a collegial learning environment. The Institute does not take a particular point of view, but rather serves as a catalyst to facilitate analysis and discussion of land use and taxation issues—to make a difference today and to help policy makers plan for tomorrow.

The Lincoln Institute of Land Policy is an equal opportunity institution.

L LINCOLN INSTITUTE
OF LAND POLICY

113 Brattle Street
Cambridge, MA 02138-3400 USA

Phone: 1-617-661-3016 x127 or 1-800-526-3873

Fax: 1-617-661-7235 or 1-800-526-3944

E-mail: help@lincolninst.edu

Web: www.lincolninst.edu